E7J

GROWTH PARTNERING

GROWTH PARTNERING

How to Build
Your Company's Profits by
Building Customer Profits

Mack Hanan

amacom

American Management Association

Library of Congress Cataloging-in-Publication Data

Hanan, Mack.
    Growth partnering : how to build your company's profits by building
customer profits / Mack Hanan. — [Enl. ed.]
        p.   cm.
    Includes index.
    ISBN 0-8144-5060-1
    1. Partnership.   2. Industries, Size of.   3. Sales management.
4. Corporate profits.   I. Title
HD38.H338   1992
658.8'1—dc20   91-36697
                                                                  CIP

Printing number

10 9 8 7 6 5 4 3 2 1

To
Franklin Brown
Who solved the problem
Of why his company should be Preferred by his
  customers
By helping to make his customers Preferred by their own
  markets.

Contents

Foreword: Growing Each Other   ix

Preface   xiii

1. Perspectives on Growth Partnering   1

2. Platforming a Growth Partnership   15

3. Positioning as a Growth Partner   25

4. Prospecting for Growth Partners   49

5. Planning a Growth Partnership   67

6. Product Developing With Growth Partners   91

7. Business Venturing With Growth Partners   103

8. Problem-Solving in Growth Partnerships   121

9. Profit-Making From Growth Partnering   133

10. Better Mousetrapping Through Growth
    Partnering   143

Index   149

Foreword: Growing Each Other

Making "Their Business" and "Your Business" Into "Our Business"

We look at our business at Southland today very differently from the way we did ten years ago. Today we have two number-one priorities. The first is the satisfaction of our customers. The second is the growth of our suppliers. These two commitments are our top priorities because they are the keys to our own growth.

We have had an advantage over many other companies of our size and international scope because we have always thought of ourselves as a service business. Our 7-Eleven retail outlets are, after all, convenience stores. But our relationships with our suppliers, while traditionally mutually profitable, were essentially transactional. They provided products and promotions for us; we provided distribution for them. Each of us was internally focused on our own business. They assumed they were giving us what we wanted. We assumed the same about ourselves. While we were far from adversarial, we were equally far from being true business partners.

In the mid 1980s, we began to understand how we could best grow. We would have to satisfy our customers more as the

Note: This foreword presents a customer's-eye view of growth partnering.

meaning of "convenience" underwent continuing change. And we would have to grow our suppliers more as their needs to retain or achieve competitive advantage were undergoing change as well. Our growth would come from how well we grew both our customers and our suppliers. If we satisfied our customers better than anyone else, more of them would shop with us more frequently for more products and services. If we grew our suppliers better than anyone else, more of them would do more business with us in order to sustain their growth; in the process, they would sustain our own.

We came to understand that by helping our suppliers to accomplish their objectives, we would, in turn, accomplish our own. As we grew them, they would grow us so that we would grow them some more. As a service company, it became clear to us that one of our most important services is supplier growth. Without sources of profitable, growing suppliers, there would be no way that we could satisfy our customers. In everything we did, we were going to have to think of ourselves as an extension of our suppliers' businesses that reached all the way up the value chain—further than they themselves could reach—to touch our mutual customers.

We began to understand that we would have to be more than good growers of our own business. We were going to have to become good growers of our suppliers' businesses. And we were going to have to teach them how to grow us in return.

As we began to plan our role as a growth partner, we followed Mack Hanan's strategies to partner with our suppliers on a proactive basis. We called them instead of waiting by the telephone for them to call us. We incorporated them into our growth partnership agenda. We shared the problems we were having with them and the costs they were aggravating for us. We told them of new and enhanced revenue opportunities we saw. We showed them how we could plan together jointly, align our strategies more closely together to maximize their growth potential, and how we could measure the results of our joint strategies.

Ten years ago, we might have defined this process as serving supplier needs. Today we define our joint processes as serving our mutual needs to grow. As a business, we have dedicated ourselves to our suppliers' partnered growth—and we have insisted that they reciprocate and dedicate themselves to growing us.

Once we began to work under the common logic of mutual growth, mutual competitive benefits became our preeminent business objectives. We began to call each other "business partners." We began to prepare our suppliers to positively affect our profits in the same way we were preparing ourselves to improve their own.

When we first put growth partnering strategies to work, we started small with one partnering team from our side working with a correlate team from a single supplier. We began to partner on improving the near-term contribution being made to our mutual growth by a single product line. From that point of departure, we have gone forward to longer term growth plans based on our changing customer base, industry and store dynamics, and our supplier's new product and business development plans.

We combined formal growth-team meetings at each of our headquarters locations with informal ad hoc meetings between individual members. We used conference rooms and conference calls and every other kind of communication in between. We made discoveries about each other's people and businesses. We overcame the up-front barriers to full disclosure, especially in the early awkwardness of sharing for the first time with each other our visions of the future—for them, their new product plans and marketing strategies; for us, what the 7-Elevens of the future might look like, what their customer demographics would be like, and what product and service mixes they might offer. In everything we shared, we had one common criterion: How could it help our mutual growth?

The single most perceptible change is that neither of us thinks that our relationship is predicated solely on moving their goods to our customers through our stores. Today we move much more information back and forth than we move goods. The information we share is based on who is buying what, when, and where, how often, and for how much. But even moving units of information back and forth about making more money with each other is secondary to moving new growth profits back and forth between ourselves.

The stream of enhanced cash flows between us and our suppliers makes one thing very clear to us. Their health is our health. Their business is our business. Our peoples' hands are the last to touch their products and our mutual customers. Their growth and our growth are, for today, tomorrow, and as far ahead as the eyes of both of us can see, forever partnered.

Walt Abele
National Marketing Development Manager
The Southland Corporation

Preface

How can you grow your business?

You cannot.

You can only grow someone else's business. His business growth will be the source of your growth. By growing, he will force growth back upon you because he will want you to grow him again.

The businesses you can grow have a name. They are called your major customers. Their growth must be the objective of your business. The capabilities you require to grow them must be your asset base.

Growth requires a partner. A growth partner is a special kind of customer. He is a customer whose costs you can significantly reduce or whose profitable sales volume you can significantly increase. In one or both of these ways, you can improve his profits. This is the basis for his growth. It is also the basis for his contribution to your own growth. As the two of you grow each other, you will become mutually indispensable.

If you cannot grow a customer, you cannot partner him. You can continue to do business with him, buying and selling, but the maximized profits of growth will elude both of you. If all your customers are buyers instead of growers, you will be a slow-growth or no-growth business. None of your customers will be growing you because you will not be growing them.

In growth partnering, each major customer powers your growth. The power of your customers can be applied coopera-

xiv Preface

tively with you so that your objectives can be the same. Each of you works to grow the other's business.

Linkage skills of this nature are the hallmark of a strategic broker whose basic capability is a capacity to add value to everything and everybody he or she touches: to people, to products, and to processes by converting them into new forms and formats that can command enhanced values. This is essentially an opportunity-seizing and problem-solving skillset that is on the lookout for two or more businesses, one of which is your own, whose mutually competitive advantage can be improved in a single stroke.

Brokers who deal in new linkages between needs and solutions, problems and opportunities, costs and benefits are creators of new wealth because they manufacture "fit." Fit brings new wealth to life or regenerates sources of existing wealth that have matured to the point that they have become misfit. If these same assets are to be made more productive, they will have to be put together in ways that will challenge the traditional sense of normal fit: ways that go by names like customized, specialized, individualized, tailored, and integrated. These words are the vocabulary of growth partnering because they are the keystone strategies for growth.

It is becoming standard practice for suppliers and their customers to share with each other such assets as product and process development technologies and sales forecasts for products that are important to both of them. In the manner of General Electric Company, an increasing number of businesses are "shifting from transactions to relationships." Depending on each company and its industry, relationship building can take a variety of forms:

- In health care, Baxter Healthcare Corporation holds "teambuilding" seminars on cost management for its customer hospitals "to help them manage their businesses more effectively."
- Xerox Corporation helps customers install quality assurance processes so that they will think of Xerox "as a partner, not just another vendor." Xerox and General Elec-

tric send their people to each other's in-house training programs to learn how their products can be better used together.

▲ Sherwin-Williams Inc. lets its customer, Sears, Roebuck Inc., select the people that Sears wants to have service its account. The two companies also make joint sales and product-turnover plans.

▲ With its smaller customers, Digital Equipment Corporation puts together corporate image programs in their local communities "to help them be successful."

Growth partnering makes having traditional customers and clients obsolete. The same is true of suppliers. Unless you can convert these two sources of your wealth—the only ones that can improve your profits—to partners, your costs of doing business with them will be unnecessarily high and your earnings unnecessarily low. If a competitor partners with them first, you may lose them as customers and suppliers, let alone partners. With no one to grow you, you will have no way to grow.

Every customer whose growth you can help maximize represents a prospective partner for you. Conversely, a partner whose growth you cannot help maximize represents an opportunity cost for both of you. It will be impossible for you to grow him enough for him to grow you the most. You will be able to reduce fewer of his critical costs or to reduce them less, or you will take longer to reduce them than someone else would. He will be unable to grow you the most or the fastest in return. A similar problem will occur if you are unable to expand his revenues or earnings either enough or fast enough. In such cases, the opportunities for both of you would be greater in partnership with someone else.

The inopportune loss of potential growth can turn out to be the margin by which you lose the competitive advantage of being your industry's low-cost supplier or high-margin leader. You may blame your partners when this happens. But it will be your choice of them that will be at fault.

There are three criteria to follow in choosing the right growth partners:

1. *Significance of profit contribution,* based on the mutual ability of the partners to reduce each other's costs and expand revenues and earnings
2. *Continuity of profit contribution,* based on perpetuating significant profits over a minimum three-year partnership cycle
3. *Growth of profit contribution,* based on increasing the annual rate of profit-making over the partnership's commercial life

In these ways, growth partnering forces you to reevaluate your customer portfolio according to profit criteria, not sales volume or account participation but earnings contribution. It also requires you to redefine your historical criteria for what constitutes a major customer and to reexamine the liabilities of not partnering with each of them.

Customers who are partnerable but who remain unpartnered will be suboptimizing your growth potential because you are still simply selling to them. In return, you will be suboptimizing their potential profits if they are still only buying from you. The same is true for your suppliers. If they are partnerable but remain unpartnered, they will also suboptimize your profits when you buy from them.

The objective of growth partnering is to grow your customers so that your customers can grow you. This means that you must learn to think of your basic sales transaction as moving improved profits to your customers, not moving products and services. It means that the drive force of your business must become the improvement of your customers' competitive advantage, not your manufacturing or marketing processes. It means that you must externalize your internal focus so that your customers dominate your vision of who you are and what you do. It means that your customer vision must be evidenced in your business mission, which should not focus on your being the best maker or servicer or supplier but on your making your customers the best competitors in their own industries. "We are in business to grow our customers," you must say in the first words of the first sentence of your mission statement.

When you are asked what you make, you must be able to say that "We make our customers grow." When you are asked what you sell, you must be able to say "We sell added competitive advantage for our customers." When you are asked to show your results, you must be able to call on your customers to testify for you. Their growth is your true bottom line as their grower.

Simply staying close to your customers is an insufficient 1980s position. Thinking of yourself in a one-way relationship being driven by your customers is similarly outdated. You must be their driver, driving your customers' growth; not just staying close to them to see where they may lead you but leading them to new and enhanced profits that they would not otherwise be able to achieve.

In order to make the most of your business opportunity to grow and be grown, your need for partners must transcend every other need of your business. You can determine whether it does by your degree of obsession with the question, *"Who can we grow and how can we grow them?"*

In the past, even though growth has always been a partnered affair, the true sources of growth often went unacknowledged because managers looked almost exclusively inward at their own businesses. Raymond Rubicam, a cofounder of Young & Rubicam Inc., could say, "I didn't build the business. I built the people who built the business." In truth, and with an acknowledgment to growth partnering, it would have been more appropriate for him to say, "I built the people who built the clients who built the business." His people were his sources of costs. They went down the elevators every night. Their clients—working around the clock twenty-four hours a day, seven days a week, all over the world to get out the products whose sales Rubicam's advertising was driving—were his sources of growth.

GROWTH PARTNERING

1

Perspectives on Growth Partnering

The only way to grow a business is to maximize earnings on sales while controlling all the costs that contribute to each sale. No company can do either of these things well enough by itself to ensure its compeitive advantage. It cannot reduce its costs enough without the help of its customers and suppliers who account for many of them. Nor can it expand its profitable sales volume enough without their help. Companies can no longer look only to their markets as their source of funds. Their suppliers must become a second source of improved profits.

Any company in its role as customer that uses its markets solely *to make money from them* and its suppliers merely *to buy products from them* is operating at a competitive disadvantage. Similarly, any company in its role as supplier that uses its customers *to make money from them* instead of *making money for them* is relinquishing competitive advantage to other suppliers whose first mission is customer profit improvement.

Customers are regularly coming to depend on their suppliers to help control the internal operating costs of their business functions and processes instead of just their costs of purchase. Suppliers are coming to see their customers rather than their own processes or products as the sources of their profits and are committing themselves to customer growth as the principal cause of their own growth.

In these ways, the roles of both customers and suppliers

are undergoing significant transformation. Each is being required to be a grower of the other. In addition to providing quality products and sevices, suppliers must be able to apply them to reduce their customers' costs or expand customer revenues and earnings. Customers, for their part, must help their suppliers control the costs of selling and serving them, and they must come to regard purchase as an investment opportunity to have their profits improved. The prices of their investments can then be related to the return they create, removing margin pressure on their suppliers that comes from cost-based pricing.

Digital Equipment Corporation is saying "We have switched from adversarial relationships to true partnerships" with suppliers. Boeing Company's version of partnering is stated this way: "Our thinking has evolved from, 'Find the guy with the lowest bid and monitor him so he doesn't screw up' to 'Find the guy who makes the best product and make him part of the process.' "

In other forms of growth partnering, suppliers are sharing in customer sales projections so their production scheduling can be more closely integrated. Suppliers are increasingly being brought into customer design conferences at the stage where there is still just "a clean sheet of paper." Some suppliers are setting up just-in-time production lines inside customer plants and customers are sponsoring college courses in statistical process control for the supplier people who work on them. Xerox sends its own teams to train suppliers to become Xerox-certified, qualifying them as business partners.

In the computer industry, erstwhile archrivals IBM and Apple Computer have created a jointly owned company, independently managed, to develop advanced software products. The coalition gives Apple access to IBM's sales and distribution system into large corporate customers. In turn, IBM gains access to Apple's software technology. The partnership acknowledges a basic truth about the computer business as well as all industries: No company can go it alone any more in developing new technology or serving customers with only partial or proprietary solutions to comprehensive operating problems. As a result, the power of any individual company has been diffused by customer insistence on open, interchangeable products and services. This enables customers to rely on a single source of supply, partner with the company or alliance that provides the source, and make market control a customer prerogative.

Even such dyed-in-the-wool competitors as the Big Three of automaking are growth partnering. In 1988 General Motors, Ford, and Chrysler created a consortium to develop composite materials for their cars and trucks. A year later, GM and Chrysler began joint manufacturing of transmission parts in an alliance called New Venture Gear. Since 1991, all three companies have been building electric batteries jointly, conducting cooperative emissions research, and working together on electronic automotive controls.

When their first partnerships began, engineers and scientists for each company were constantly running back to their managers to check on how much information they should share. It took a gestation period of about nine months before they could get comfortable working together. Now that they are, time and expenses are being cut in half.

In the 1990s, any supplier who is content to sell products or services solely on their price and performance and let it go at that, and any customer who buys them that way, will be doing business in the slow lane. Maintaining multiple vendors is no more affordable as a strategy for maximizing competitiveness than making something for everybody and selling anything to anybody. Multiple vendors can never know enough about a customer's business to reduce his operating costs or expand his revenues and earnings to the fullest. No customer can share his business needs fully enough with any of them. Nor can a customer who has many suppliers ever know enough about how to take full advantage of any one supplier's capabilities to increase his growth.

As customers and suppliers are forced to become more selective in doing business with each other and as their reasons for doing business undergo change—quality of profit improvement coming before product or service quality; return on a purchase investment coming before price—the traditional buyer-seller relationship of business undergoes changes. It moves from win-lose to win-win; from adversaries to allies; from supplier and customer to partners.

Partners are companies that come together to grow each other as the best way to grow themselves. A supplier partner envisions himself as a grower of his customers rather than as a manufacturer or marketer. A customer partner envisions himself as a grower of his suppliers rather than as a buyer and user of their products or services.

Growth partnering has given the concept of "managing accounts" a new meaning. It no longer has to do with the ability to load up a customer with products. Now it means growing your business partner by growing your contribution to his profits. His forecasting, manufacturing, and inventory problems become your concern, not just his. Unless you both solve them, the account will go out of control and neither of you will be able to maximize profits.

Allies who can be growth partners, not merely customers or suppliers, are the new demand. In an increasing number of customer organizations, the word is out: Cut back on the number of suppliers you deal with; cut back on the number of their people who call on you; cut back on the number of requests for proposal that you send out and the number of bids you get back; cut back on your costs of buying, the number of people you employ in your purchasing functions, and the amount of fixed costs you allocate to them.

At the same time, suppliers are cutting back on the number of markets they want to be in and the number of customers they want to do business with in each market. They are cutting back on the number of requests for proposal they bid on and they are learning to say "No, thank you" to unprofitable business that they would normally have taken just to get the volume.

In every industry, the customer-supplier relationship is being reduced to a small number of strategic allies doing business with each other in each important area of their business. In manufacturing industries, some customers are approaching the ideal of having one dedicated supplier for every part number and no more than two partners for every commodity.

There was once a time when General Motors could take

pride in saying that there were only two kinds of people in the world: Those who worked for GM and those who sold to it. At that stage of its life, GM did business with over 5,000 suppliers. In the 1980s, it set about to reduce them by half and then by half again in the 1990s until only about 1,000 are left.

For Toyota, this is still too many. Toyota concentrates its business with only 250 suppliers while the Big Three of the United States, although cutting back, are still dealing with thousands. This gives Toyota the advantage of being able to partner in depth all along its supply chain, coaching and counseling its suppliers in how to squeeze more costs out of their own operations and Toyota's operations as well. Each Toyota automobile ends up costing between $500 and $1,000 less than its Big Three competitors as a result.

These savings come from reduced incoming inspection and testing costs, lower costs for scrap and rework and warranty fulfillment, and greater control of inventory costs from better forecasting and closer integration of manufacturing with supplier delivery-cycle times.

McDonald's is another company that is growth partnering with its suppliers. In each of its regions, it is allied with single-source suppliers. All by itself this accelerates McDonald's growth. With fewer contacts and longer lead times with each of them, McDonald's can plan jointly with its reduced supply base. There is also a freer feeling about sharing proprietary data with its partners so that they can counsel together on reducing their mutual costs of doing business and take fuller advantage of opportunities to enhance mutual profits.

If you and your customers are not partnering with each other as mutual growth sources, your customers may put it to you like this: "Grow us or we will grow ourselves at your expense." Retailing is an example. Supermarketers and discounters who do not have the benefits of being grown by their supplier partners are trying to get equivalent benefits. With their nonpartners, merchants are demanding slotting allowances before they award them shelf space and failure fees to protect themselves against the costs of stocking new products that turn out to be unsuccessful.

Buying Into Partnering

At the outset, every growth partnership represents an added cost. This cost is the counterpart of the startup cost of a new business whose up-front investment represents negative cash flow that continues until a return on the investment can be earned. Potential partners could properly greet each other with the salutation, "Hello, incremental cost." This is what partners must be prepared to pay for growth. But it is not what they buy.

When one partner takes on another, each buys into a stream of future cash flows that are greater, or that can be realized sooner, or are more certain than the alternatives of going it alone or with another partner. When a partner buys the ability of another company to accelerate the growth of his business, he is contracting for one or more of the following capabilities.

- ▲ Current sales will turn over faster.
- ▲ Future sales will come on stream sooner, in larger volume or with higher earnings, or with greater certainty.
- ▲ Current costs will be reduced.
- ▲ Some future costs will be avoidable in part or in whole.

Any of these results of partnering will improve a partner's competitive advantage and accelerate his growth. Yet not all of them are created equal. Cost control is a vital contribution of partnership. New products, processes, or projects too costly for one partner alone can become affordable for both together. Even the elimination of current shared costs that a partnership can make partially redundant for each partner is a worthy basis for an alliance. But cost control, crucial as it is, can only support major growth. Expanded business opportunities, represented by increased sales, must be the compelling reason to partner. In the final analysis, it is what partners buy from each other.

Companies are in business to grow. Growth is based on earnings accumulation, not cost savings. New cash flows that are genuinely new—that come from the commercialization of new business entities, new products and services, or from the penetration of new markets or the enhanced penetration of current markets in new ways—are the heart and soul of partnering. They build new revenue bases for businesses, providing burgeoning platforms to realize the full extension of existing market shares or the cultivation of entirely unexplored areas of expanded opportunities.

"Where are you taking your business?" is the question that begins each partnership's dialogue. "How can we help you get there?" is the second question. What mix of our expertise and experience, our processes and products, our funds and facilities, our operational smarts and our market smarts will accelerate the achievement of your objectives and help ensure their realization? What can be done to help you exceed them—to boost your goals exponentially—so that you can stand on your three-year horizon twenty-four months from now instead of thirty-six?

As you ask these questions, your own growth will be implicit in their answers. With every dollar's worth of growth that you contribute to a partner, what are you buying for yourself? By comparing what you invest in the growth of a partner with what you get out of it, you can calculate your *return on investment (ROI) in partnered growth*. A partnership's ROI will prove its cost-effectiveness for you. Before you calculate it, figure it out for your partner. What is his ROI in partnered growth with you? Unless he agrees that this is a "good number," there will be no point in calculating your own. If the numbers are mutually good, you can look forward to buying into a robust partnership. Otherwise the ROIs will warn you if there is a wimp in the deal.

Structuring a Partnership

Growth partnerships are based on a four-part structure: a single stretch objective, a minimal strategy mix to achieve it, win-win rewards, and controlled risk. Each part has the same first name—*mutual.*

1. The *mutual objective* of every partnership must be to maximize a customer's growth. When a supplier and a customer partner together, the customer's growth must come first. When two or more suppliers join together in partnership, the end result must be to grow their common customers or they will never be able to grow themselves or each others as partners.

2. The *mutual strategy* of every partnership is to achieve the partnered objective by sharing minimal resources over minimal time. Minimal resources keep costs down and let the partners operate at a low break-even rate. Minimal time ensures minimal opportunity loss.

3. The *mutual reward* of every partnership is that both partners grow more and faster and with greater certainty than they could otherwise grow, either alone or with another partner.

4. The *mutual sharing of risk* enables partners to guard against opportunity loss, which is the greatest threat to partnership. The principal danger is always that the partners will fail to achieve the opportunity represented by their growth objective, the very reason for the partnership's existence. If the objective is lost, the resources allocated to the partnership's strategy are also lost. The irreplaceable loss will always be time.

Structuring the Partnered Objective

Partnerships are profit maximizers. That is how the partners grow each other and, in turn, themselves. The volume of incremental profits that they generate is paramount. Earning profits in volume is maximizing growth. Earning profits quickly and recurrently is further maximizing growth by minimizing the time within which growth takes place. The time value of money as well as its dollar value must be recognized in the objective of partners who agree to increase each other's wealth.

The certainty of growth is the most difficult factor to calculate in a partnership. It will be evidenced in the way that the specific strategies the partners choose to focus on match the customer partner's profit problems and opportunities with the supplier partner's capacity to solve some of the problems and capitalize on some of the opportunities.

Growth partners share the same needs. They each need to maximize new profits and they need to be able to count on a continuing flow of profits with plannable certainty. This motivation brings them together in partnership. Because the method by which partners prosper is for both of them to grow the customer partner, they must always acknowledge it as the sole source of partnered growth.

The growth objective for a customer partner can be broken down into two component parts. Part one is profit growth from solving cost problems in the customer's operations. Which business functions will compose the partnership's arena? Which of their costs? By how much will they be reduced? Part two is profit growth from capitalizing on sales opportunities for the customer. Which markets will compose the partnership's arena? Which product lines sold to them? By how much will their revenues and earnings be increased?

Only after the customer's composite profit objective has been planned can the supplier partner plan his own growth objective.

The customer's objective is his return on the investment he makes in growth partnering. The supplier's growth will be financed by that investment. The customer's return must maximize his use of money; it must be a good deal. Similarly, the investment that the customer makes in the supplier constitutes the supplier's return. It must maximize the supplier's use of money so that it represents a good deal for him too.

Successful growth partnerships are successful because they are a good deal for both partners. Each wins. If only one can win, there is no basis for partnership.

Structuring the Partnered Strategy

The partnered objective quantifies *how much* profit will be improved. Partnered strategy specifies *how, where,* and *when* a cost will be reduced or revenues improved in the customer business to which the supplier is going to apply his capabilities.

Cost reduction strategies require agreement on the selection of customer business functions where economies can be introduced, freeing funds for other uses. Proposing cost reduction presupposes knowledge of how a customer's costs are generated: labor costs, work flow processing costs, materials costs, manufacturing costs, sales and distribution costs, communications costs—whatever costs the supplier can affect. If cost reduction is going to be part of a supplier's contribution to a partnership, the supplier must be expert in the customer's operations.

Revenue improvement strategies require agreement on the selection of customer markets in which sales can be increased to bring in new funds. Proposing revenue gain presupposes knowledge of how turnover of a customer's existing products can be increased or penetration stepped up for his new products. If revenue gain is going to be contributed to a partnership, a supplier must be expert in customer sales development.

When customers ask a supplier candidate for partnership how he proposes to grow their businesses, they are asking him to position himself as a grower. Does he propose to grow them in the role of a cost reducer? If so, what does he know of their current costs; how much and how soon can he reduce them? Or does he propose to grow them in the role of a sales developer? If so, what does he know of their current sales; how much and how soon can he expand them?

The supplier's answers to these questions will be his growth proposals. Each proposal will make three statements: Here is something I know about your business, either a function that is overcosted by my standards or a market that my standards indicate is being undersold. This is how much added growth I can bring to it. Here is how and when I can do it.

Market share growth is volume growth. The dollar value of each successive share of market reaches an optimal point and then undergoes diminishing returns as the costs to push beyond that point rise in disproportion to their yield. Growth through a customer's sales function can be complicated by the inverse relationships between the incremental costs of volume and the incremental profits that can be made from new revenues.

In contrast, reducing a customer's costs to improve his profit is relatively straightforward. Dollar for dollar, reduced costs can often drop undiminished to the bottom line.

Structuring Partnered Control

Partners must set up a control system to monitor the partnership's achievement on a progressive basis. Attaining each milestone "on plan" announces that the partnership is working.

Strategy can be measured—or, for that matter, managed—only if it is explicit. It is not a strategy just to "reduce inventory cost." How will it be done: Will labor or materials costs be reduced? Or will insurance costs, security costs, energy costs, or the costs of capital be the expenses that will be brought down? How will that happen? Will materials handling be automated to be more cost-effective or will space requirements be reduced or will turnover be increased? By how much? Within what time frame?

Control must be planned before partnering begins as well as after. Risk can be minimized by answering five questions in advance of proposing a partnership:

1. Is this customer a good bet for partnering because he is being grown significantly by me right now or is growable?
2. Is this customer's business susceptible to significant cost reduction or is his market susceptible to significant revenue improvement?
3. Is this objective significant to the customer rather than merely achievable?
4. Is this strategy minimal in cost yet capable of maximizing achievement of the objective?
5. Is this control system capable of early warning of failure?

A sixth question relates to the specific risk of the supplier: Will his own objective be significant enough commensurate with his risk? Otherwise, the supplier may be forsaking business for philanthropy.

Perfecting the "Full Linda"

A partner in place tends to remain in place. This makes partnerships self-perpetuating, armoring them with an invulnerability to competition from would-be third parties and, over time, elevating a partnered relationship to the status of an indispensable alliance. At IBM, this phenomenon is called the Linda Effect, after a classical growth partner.

Linda represents the supplier half of a supplier-customer partnership. Each year she manages the partnership so that it grows the customer more than the year before. She does this by a rollover three-year growth plan that is composed of a menu of profit improvement projects. The projects are quantified, time-framed, and teamed from both sides. Linda's presentation of each three-year plan goes like this:

> This year's three-year growth plan proposes a cumulative net profit of $7.75 million. As Figure 1-1 shows, three profit improvement projects in year one will account for $1.5 million. There will be four profit improvement projects in each of years two and three that will account for $2.5 million and $3.75 million, respectively. In year two, one project will be a migration of a project begun in year one. Three of the four projects in year three will be migrations from year two. Your investment in each migration will be fully funded by the previous year's earnings, enabling you to capitalize the migrated project with the cash flows of our partnership's money rather than your own operating funds.

If Linda were your competitor, how would you departner her?

In order to get a preliminary hearing, you would have to

Figure 1-1. Three-year growth plan.

Three-Year Accumulated Profit Improvement	$7,750,000
Year One Total Profit Improvement	$1,500,000
Project 1	750,000
Project 2	450,000
Project 3	300,000
Year Two Total Profit Improvement	$2,500,000
Project 1	800,000
Project 2	700,000
Project 3	650,000
Project 4	350,000
Year Three Total Profit Improvement	$3,750,000
Project 1	1,250,000
Project 2	1,000,000
Project 3	800,000
Project 4	700,000

propose a greater or quicker or surer flow of partnered funds. If you said that these would come from a lower price, you would have to show how deep a discount you would have to give to exceed the customer's proposed profits from partnering with Linda. If you claimed product superiority, you would have to translate your product's performance benefits into greater profit benefits than Linda's, and if you based your case on being a more profitable partner, you would have to start the bidding over and above Linda's proposed $7.75 million for three years of partnering. Otherwise, from the customer's point of view, why bother?

Linda will tend to stay in place no matter what you propose as long as the partnership of which she is a part has a track record of previous success and her partner feels assured of its continuing success. Linda's partner has everything to lose and little or nothing that can neutralize the loss by switching partners. In the worst-case scenario, Linda's partner could lose the partnership's projected $7.75 million over the next three years. He could also lose the invested value of each year's cash flows, some of which was going to be used to pay for the next year's projects. But most important of all, he could lose Linda and the future value of her forthcoming contributions to the growth of the partnership.

Even under a best-case scenario, you will see how the Full Linda that your competitor has perfected—the partnership equivalent of the full nelson stranglehold in wrestling—makes Linda's possession of a partnered position nine-tenths of the law of account control. Even if her customer suspects that you could grow his business better than Linda, which means you could grow it more or faster and just as surely, how much more would you have to propose to make it a fair trade: a third more than Linda's three-year proposal of $7.75 million in only two-thirds the time, or two-thirds more in one-third the time? Could you guarantee what could essentially amount to a total of $15 million based on principal, interest, and consideration for opportunity cost?

If you can answer yes to questions such as these you will be taking on the supreme challenge: to propose to do better than an incumbent partner who is operating from an interior position of strength, who knows the customer and has open access to key customer managers and their proprietary data. When you make your proposal, you know in advance what will happen. Linda will be given the courtesy of matching the offer. She does not have to duplicate it. All she needs to do is to negate it or come close. As the partner in place, she will tend to remain in place. You, as the pretender, will continue to pretend that you should replace her.

2

Platforming a
Growth Partnership

When you set out to partner, you have two options:

1. You can partner one-on-one with a customer.
2. You can enhance your partnerability by allying with one or more other suppliers before you partner with a customer.

One-on-one partnering can be your strategy of choice when your own capabilities are sufficient for a customer's growth. If they are not, you can expand them with the capabilities of other suppliers who can supplement or complement your strengths and make up for your weaknesses. In the process of multisupplier partnering, each supplier will inevitably help to grow the others. But their mutual customer's growth will always be the drive force behind it.

Suppliers come together in partnership when a customer common to them says, in effect, that no one of them can grow him enough or fast enough with only his own products and services. As a result, two basic types of supplier-plus-supplier partnerships can come about: complementary partners and supplementary partners. Each represents the resolution of a "make-or-partner" decision in favor of partnering.

1. *Complementary Partners.*
   ▲ *Product and Product.* The product of one partner can

be complemented by the products of others to form a
single-source, comprehensive integrated system.

▲ *Product and Service*. The product of one partner can be
complemented by the application, consultation, and
educational services of others to form a single-source
solution system.

▲ *Product and Sales Force*. The product of one partner can
be complemented by the sales force or distributors of
another to provide market access for the product supplier and an enhanced single-source capability for the
sales force or distribution supplier.

2. *Supplementary Partners*. The technology of one partner
can supplement the technology of another to give new
or enhanced capability to generate scientific break-
throughs in developing new processes or new products.
Technology partnerships can take the forms of rsearch
and development (R&D) partnerships, joint ventures, or
multipartner consortiums.

Partnering between suppliers has three possible directions:
up, down, and across. A small company will probably do most
of its partnering up and across. A midsize or large company
has the freedom to partner in all three dirctions. Nonetheless,
midsize companies most often partner laterally with midsize
peers. Large companies are most likely to partner laterally or
with smaller, uniquely innovative or vertically niched businesses.

Each option has plusses and minuses. In spite of potential
drawbacks, certain types of alliances are preordained. Small
companies that need financial support, market access, or simply
a recognition of their future value must consider partnering
up. Conversely, large companies must consider partnering
down when they need technology, a ticket of entry into a specialized market, knowledge of an emergent new industry, or an
entrepreneurial shot in the arm.

Midsize companies need each other. Peer partnering
among them becomes necessary when large competitors
threaten to invade their market segments, when they can no

longer match their large competitors' clout in R&D, manufacturing, or distribution, or when they need economies of scale in order to control their costs.

Small companies have advantages of smallness such as being focused, flexible, inventive, and unabashed by tradition. They need advantages of bigness: adequate capitalization, market access and acceptance, and the privilege to make mistakes and still survive. When small businesses partner up, these are the competitive advantages they seek.

In return, large companies need advantages of smallness. They need to be more innovative. They need more of a one-to-one relationship with their customers and the ability to zero in on a market segment and become its standard of performance. These are the competitive advantages that large corporations can obtain by partnering down.

Midsize companies have fewer of the advantages of smallness than a small company but almost as many of the disadvantages. Similarly, they have fewer of the advantages of largeness than a large company but almost as many of the disadvantages. Partnering with each other is their best chance to reduce or compensate for some of these disadvantages and gain more advantages of bigness.

Partnering by a Small Supplier

Growth partnerships give small companies the chance to act big. They also allow small businesses to grow without dealing away their autonomy, which is the drive force of their inventiveness.

Small companies become partnerable when they reach the point of insufficient capitalization to support further growth and cannot go to capital markets for secondary mezzanine financing. Partnerability also becomes an option of choice when a small company has topped out its original growth curve and is stumped for ways to extend its technology by asking "What else can we sell?" or to extend its markets by asking "Who else can we sell to?"

Large companies make it a point to keep their eyes on the small players in a new industry. As soon as one large company partners with a smaller one, all the other small companies in the industry become partnerable out of self-preservation. Most large companies make minority investments when they partner down with a smaller company. In return for their money, they typically get the right to influence the small company's research and an option to grow their investment to a majority holding and make a buyout at some time in the future.

IBM and General Motors hold their initial investments in small companies at a 15 to 20 percent maximum. With an investment of this size, IBM funded Metaphor Computer Systems at the $10 million level to gain access to Metaphor's decision-support software and applications skills. In turn, IBM provided marketing support that extended Metaphor's market reach and endowed it with IBM's imprimatur. IBM later bought out Metaphor.

Genex Corporation and Genentech Inc., two microbiology suppliers, became partnerable by Monsanto when they needed funds for further product development and new market entry. Monsanto acted as their banker and consultant, at the same time finding out as an insider what the biotechnology business was all about. Several years later, Monsanto felt comfortable enough about the business to acquire G. D. Searle. In much the same way, AT&T traded a $5 million equity investment in Omnical Corporation, a small computer-aided design (CAD) manufacturer, along with R&D funds and equipment discounts, for a chance to learn the CAD business.

In similar fashion, General Motors has partnered with Teknowledge Inc., a manufacturer of software for factory production scheduling and automobile design. GM has hedged its bet by also partnering with other software developers. Teknowledge, for its part, does the same with several large companies that, like GM, are also its equity investors.

If you are a small company, you can help a large company grow in seven ways by providing:

1. Innovative or breakthrough technology that the larger company cannot develop on its own, either as a source

of new products or to supplement or complement the state of the art of the larger company's existing technologies

2. Products for the larger company to market, either to round out its current lines or extend them into new markets
3. Access to your specialized market niche
4. Insights to the larger company of what your type of business and its industry are all about
5. A training ground for the larger company's managers, either in entrepreneurial management strategy in general or your industry in particular, or both
6. Specialized applications skills
7. A high-return investment opportunity

In return, the larger company you partner with can help you grow in three ways by providing:

1. Capital funds
2. Marketing support in sales, sales promotion and advertising, and distribution
3. Repute by association

Partnering by a Large Supplier

Large companies become partnerable with each other when they require additional technologies or marketing capabilities in order to sell comprehensive, integrated product and service systems to their major customers. IBM has allied with MCI Communications to add MCI's telecommunications technologies to IBM's information networks. IBM also partners with the Boeing Company to acquire systems integration expertise. At the same time, IBM is teaming with some of its largest customers to remarket their IBM applications to other companies in each customer's market.

In many cases, just the fact that a large company is large makes it partnerable. As industries mature, their major players all encounter many aspects of the same syndrome: growth slows, margins shrink, costs rise, breakthrough innovation winds down or stops, and competitors consolidate. It becomes increasingly difficult to start successful high-growth businesses internally from scratch. When global competitors appear, managers find as they did at Boeing that "It is no longer realistic for us to go it alone." Boeing partners product-to-product all over the world with other large companies—in Japan, Italy, and wherever else it can find high-quality subcontractors—to provide parts for its commercial airliners. These partnerships reduce Boeing's financial exposure and, at the same time, lower its current costs.

If you are a large company, you can help a smaller company grow in three ways, by providing (1) capital funds, (2) marketing support, and (3) repute.

In return, the smaller company you partner with can help you grow in seven ways by providing:

1. Innovative or breakthrough technology that you cannot develop on your own, and the help you need to build a learning curve in it early in its emergence, either as a source of new products or to supplement or complement the state of the art of your existing technologies
2. New products for you to market, either to round out your current lines or extend them into new markets
3. Access to a specialized market niche
4. Insights into a new type of business and industry to help you decide whether you want to enter it
5. A training ground for your managers in entrepreneurial management strategies or in an emergent new industry, or both
6. Specialized applications skills
7. An investment opportunity for your venture capital

Partnering by a Midsize Supplier

Midsize companies become partnerable when they start to get squeezed from the top by larger companies with more cash and lower costs and from the bottom by smaller, higher technology niche marketers. As Unisys, a midsize computer maker, has experienced, companies in the middle of their industries can go two ways: "Become full-service international players or subsuppliers to the big guys." The first option takes money. The second option requires significant psychological readjustment and physical downsizing. Partnering offers a third course.

A large part of a midsize company's untenability comes from being unable to match "the big guys" dollar for dollar in R&D. Another liability is comparatively skimpy market coverage and customer service. To remain in the middle of the pack resigns a business to being outdeveloped, outproduced, outdistributed, outsold, and outadvertised, and all at greater cost-effectiveness and economies of scale.

Partnering allows midsize companies to become in effect big, so they can continue to participate in the sciences and markets of their chief skills. When the giant money-center banks began to broaden their base from major metropolitan areas into the provinces of regional banks, two and sometimes three or more of the regionals started partnering. As allies, they form a single superregional bank that may control as much as 80 percent of their region's assets. The superregionals are integrating their information systems, exchanging market information, creating new products their customers are asking for, and handling major projects simultaneously. By partnering, they are avoiding overextending their managers, their financial resources, and their own organizations.

If you are a midsize company, you can help another midsize company grow—and grow you—in four ways, by providing:

1. Supplementary products and capabilities that reinforce each other
2. New capabilities that can extend the reach and degree of existing lines of business in a "buy vs. make" manner
3. Relief from duplicated costs
4. The critical mass necessary to gain parity in purchasing, distribution, and other marketing strategies, and to give the partners first call on attracting superior managers

Pairing off Internationally

In Europe, spurred by the Common Market, suppliers are acquiring other companies of their same size and smaller across formerly sacrosanct national borders. They are becoming transnational because the megacorporations that threaten them are also global in nature. To become world class themselves, they are choosing to relinquish some of their nationalism for the sake of stronger research and development, economies of scale, extended marketing capabilities, and cost savings from the elimination of duplicate product lines and processes.

Joint ventures, takeovers, and minority-stake acquisitions are occurring not only within the twelve nations of the European Community but also between EC and non-Community companies. The joint venture between the Netherlands' Philips and Great Britain's General Electric is an example of pairing within the EC. Outside, Sweden's ASEA and BBC Brown Boveri of Switzerland have become an electrical equipment partnership that makes products for the entire European continental market. They manage their combined business in the "American style" with emphasis on profits and use English as their common language.

The jointly owned company, called ABB, for ASEA Brown Boveri, now ranks with General Electric, Westinghouse, Siemens, Hitachi, Mitsubishi, and Toshiba. This is a marked contrast to the positions of the two companies before their partnership. ASEA was trying to develop profitable niche businesses "between the cracks" of the megacorporations. Brown Boveri, meanwhile, was retrenching to its base operations in the conventional power generation and distribution businesses after an expensive fling in nuclear power.

In the case of ASEA and Brown Boveri, both of which are in mature industries, their main product lines had become commodities with no compelling differentiation except price. Competitors in their industries typically buy more business than they sell. Coming together may therefore be the only alternative to falling apart. To be a permanent member of a second tier of companies that can neither compete for major customers nor defend their own customers from missionary penetration by larger competitors is to be consigned to a commercial limbo. Fight through combination, or flight through downsizing or divestiture, are the only ways out.

The airline industry is another example of international alliances. Half a dozen airlines are coming to dominate European business. These megalines will be true international carriers whose consolidated route structures and reservation systems will force all other airlines into accommodation with them. Lufthansa is one such megaline. Scandinavian Airlines System (SAS), a midsize competitor, was presented with two options. One was to become integrated into Lufthansa's sytem as a feeder to Lufthansa passengers in Germany who might want to fly to Scandinavia. Its other option was to form global alliances with airlines that have compatible flight schedules, computerized reservation systems, hotels, and other service subsidiaries. This is the option SAS has taken, forming alliances with Thai Airways, Continental Airlines, All Nippon Airways, Swissair, Finnair, and several smaller airlines and international hotel chains. For SAS, which is only the eighth-ranking airline in Europe and nineteenth in the world, its alliances give it a global presence as a worldwide marketer as well as economies of a scale otherwise available only to a megacarrier.

3

Positioning as a Growth Partner

The overriding commitment of every manager is to "grow the business." When growth stops, or even when the rate of growth slows down, maturity occurs. Maturity signals that a business has run out of customers to grow or that it has run out of strategies to grow them. If it has run out of growable customers, the business needs new markets. If it has run out of strategies to grow them, it needs new marketers. The third alternative is to accept decline.

Accepting decline is the death wish for a business. Supplier managers who choose life are always on the lookout for customers who can contribute a specific number of dollars to them every year. Customers are looking, too. They are searching for suppliers who can save them a specific amount of money or help them make more. Finding partners to grow and finding ways to grow them is what their concept of being in business is all about. Taking this stance is the only viable business position. If your customers are growing slowly or not at all, so will you. If they become depressed or recessed, so will you. If they fail, it will be at least in part because you failed to grow them. With every customer you lose, a source of your own growth goes as well.

What, then, is your single most precious resource? It is customers whose businesses you can grow so that they will grow you in return. What is your single most precious asset? It is your expertise in growing your customers' businesses so that they will be better growers of your own business.

The main difference between a fast-growth business and a slow-growth or no-growth business is in their asset bases. Slow-growth businesses cultivate product and process managers who are experts in making quality products. Fast-growth businesses cultivate managers who are experts in making quality profits for their customers. Product managers set out to grow their products. Growth managers set out to grow the customers who will grow their products.

Product managers build product lines. Growth managers build the markets for them. They are the ones who are positioned for growth partnering.

Grasping the Two Handles of Growth

When you are in position to grow a customer's business, you hold the two handles of growth. One handle enables you to reduce customer costs. The other handle enables you to expand customer revenues and earnings.

Your search for costs that you can reduce in the customer operations that you affect must be unceasing. Some of these costs will come from a customer's own functions. The rest will be costs that a customer incurs in doing business with you. Every dollar you can reduce will help make a customer more competitive as a lower cost supplier. Even pennies make worthy cost-saving objectives. Phillips Petroleum Company is an example. Each of its managers once supervised 5.8 workers. By bringing the number up to 7.3 workers, Phillips reduced its management costs from 30 cents to 28 cents a payroll dollar.

Even though customer cost reduction must always be one part of your partnering strategy, cost reduction alone will not maximize a customer's competitiveness. Profitable new sales are the mother lode of growth. Many of the dollars you can free up from a customer's costs can be reinvested in sales development so that you can be your customers' *market maker.*

Making markets is the key to partnered growth. Your customers' growth comes from their customers. Your growth is a second derivative of their growth, passed along to you through your customers from their markets. This tells you what it means to grasp the growth handle marked sales development. In order to be positioned as a sales development partner with your customers, you must help them become sales development partners with their own customers.

When you grow customers and help them grow customers of their own, you can apply your two growth handles to any one of five capabilities:

1. You can use your *product or process technology* to expand customer revenues through innovation or developmental applications expertise or to reduce customer costs through process re-engineering.
2. You can use your *manufacturing* capability to expand customer revenues by adding quality to products or adding products to lines of business or to reduce customer costs by reducing production downtime, scrap, or warranty expenses.
3. You can use your *marketing* capability to expand customer revenues by penetrating new markets, adding distribution channels or sales force coverage, or to reduce customer costs by product cross-selling and market consolidation.
4. You can use your *information technology* to expand customer revenues by coordinating marketing and manufacturing, market data basing, and sales tracking or to reduce customer costs by condensing product development cycles and controlling inventory just in time with manufacturing scheduling and sales demand.
5. You can use your *strategic planning* capability to accelerate customer penetration into emergent growth opportunities or to reduce customer opportunity costs from entering unpromising markets or entering promising markets with too little too late.

In any of these areas, you and a partner can grasp the growth handles together by combining capabilities, or one partner can turn a handle for the other. A third option is to set up a third-party operation that is jointly sponsored by the partners that can turn the handles in their mutual behalf.

Offering Partnerable Propositions

You can go partnering for supplier allies with propositions like these:

- ▲ What if we can give you access to new products, to high-quality products near or at the zero-defects level, or to products that can round out your current lines, open new markets for you or give you added competitive advantages with the customers in your installed base or penetrate new markets?
- ▲ What if we can give you added sales coverage or expanded distribution, open new channels for you, or help you maximize your clout with existing channels, give your sales force more to sell or more access to high-level customers to sell it to or more value to add to each sale?

Daimler-Benz is one of many companies that is reaching out to other suppliers all over the world with partnering propositions like these: In the United States, Daimler partners with United Technologies Corporation to grow a joint business in jet aircraft; in France, it partners with Aerospatiale S.A. to grow a helicopter business; and in Japan, it partners with Mitsubishi to grow a business in aerospace. These partnerships make Daimler-Benz a global company, no longer merely German, in the same way that United Technologies is no longer "American," Aerospatiale is no longer "French," and Mitsubishi is no longer "Japanese."

Mega-alliances that are as extremely cross-cultural as Mitsubishi–Daimler-Benz are not easy and are frequently uneasy. On the German side, the feeling has been expressed that "the effort expended in getting to know each other has been greater than expected." One of the solutions proposed by the Japanese is that "We've got to stop acting so Japanese and they've got to stop acting so German." Since it is unlikely that the Germans will ever become sufficiently Japanese to suit the Japanese, nor will the Japanese become suitably German, a third culture is being created in their alliances that is "neither yet both" and unlikely to exist anywhere else in the world. Such international alliances will be truly Third World enterprises.

Air France and Lufthansa are partners in jointly marketing their airline services, coordinating their schedules and routes, training each other's pilots, and sharing common airport facilities. Swissair and Scandinavian Airlines also partner to coordinate routes and schedules yet go even further to share 10 percent of each other's stock. Sabena, Belgium's airline, has a dual partnership with British Airways and KLM Royal Dutch Airlines where each has a 20 percent ownership stake in Sabena.

In mass retailing, retailers and their suppliers are coming to agree with Warner-Lambert that "To get to the consumer, you have to do it together." Procter & Gamble (P&G) sees it the same way: "The major retailers around the world are moving toward cooperative alliances with a select few suppliers. We must be one of them." The P&G strategy to become "alliance material" is to become the most desirable supplier to deal with.

In order to achieve its objective, P&G is asking such questions as:

- How much will it help our retailers if both our companies use the same stock-keeping number to identify each item, eliminating the retailer's cost to reticket each shipping container when it arrives?
- How much will it help our retailers if we ship orders just in time, according to their forecasted sales, so that smaller inventories can be maintained while still avoiding stockouts?
- How much will it help our retailers if we increase our on-time deliveries from 94 percent to 95 percent? From 95 percent to 96 percent? From 96 percent to 99.5 percent?

Growth partnering is revolutionizing the way that Procter & Gamble does business. Historically, P&G and its retailer customers were adversaries. Each spent its time asking, "How can I transfer as much of my cost as possible?" As partners, they ask how they can save each other costs by cutting inventories, smoothing out production and promotion schedules, and solving service and quality problems that affect them both. In these ways, they are obtaining many of the same benefits that industrial companies are receiving from their partners.

P&G and its retailers are basing their partnerships on three strategies:

1. Upgrade the relationship levels between them from being solely dependent on sales representatives and buyers dealing with each other on this week's margins and next week's order size to mutual profit improvement planning through Consultative Selling™ strategies.*
2. Partner on a multifunction team basis. Under each team's managing partner, typical functions include:
   ▲ Data
   ▲ Sales
   ▲ Purchasing
   ▲ Finance
   ▲ Distribution

Team activities are concerned with coordinating orders and delivery schedules on a just-in-time basis, timing the introduction of new products, correlating inventory with promotions, and reducing trucking and warehouse costs.

At Procter & Gamble, teams partner with retail customers on setting up error-free order entry systems, standardizing order processing and invoicing, and issuing electronic payments to ensure cash flows. By automating resupply, P&G has been able to reduce its inventory held by customer stores by as much as 80 percent. At Wal-Mart, the P&G inventory of Tide has been cut from thirty days to two. With smaller reorders and more frequent deliveries, P&G benefits from smoothing its production cycles. Wal-Mart benefits by not having to borrow to finance

*Consultative Selling is a registered trademark of Mack Hanan.

its P&G inventory since each order's sales pay for the next re-order.

P&G and Wal-Mart became partners after not liking each other's ways of doing business at first. For other suppliers, the transition from selling to partnering with Wal-Mart has come easier. At consumer products manufacturer Dial Corporation, Wal-Mart's partnering strategy has changed the way companies like it do business. Years ago, they prayed for orders to come from their customers. Today, they are partners who are re-garded as allies of Dial, just as Dial is regarded as an ally of theirs.

Wal-Mart partners with many of its suppliers in their de-velopment of products for it to sell and the promotions to help sell them. Starting from the concept stage, Wal-Mart encour-ages suppliers who partner with it to create new products and displays for testing in its three experimental stores in North Carolina, Arkansas, and Wisconsin. If the products catch on, Wal-Mart expands their testing to 50 more stores. As the goods move, their manufacturers "can know tomorrow what we sold today" on daily computer printouts that correlate sales, reor-der, and shipping information. When this type of constant monitoring reveals problems, Wal-Mart buyers and their part-ners go to work to change product designs, cut manufacturing costs, or improve shipping dates.

High-technology industries are becoming partnered for growth because it is too costly to fail by "missing a curve" in watching a technological breakthrough go by. Paradoxically, it has become equally costly and often unaffordable to succeed. High tech is accordingly full of joint ventures, strategic alli-ances, minority investments, and even a consortium called Se-matech that pools scientific talent from several member com-panies to conduct basic R&D and materials research in semiconductors.

Supplier-customer partnerships and supplier-supplier alli-ances are becoming the basic competitive units in all major in-dustries. Most companies will have multiple alliances. A single business such as Southland Corporation, owner of 7-11 stores, may end up as an ally with several of its major suppliers for whom it is the largest customer as they are its largest suppliers. The suppliers may also partner with each other to coordinate complementary product lines or joint promotions in 7-11 stores.

In the cooperative competition of the 1990s, partnerships will compete against partnerships. A customer and his supplier partners, allied with each supplier's own partners, will team up against other similarly partnered teams. Many teams will be ad hoc, put together based on the best players for each task. Choices will be based on each partner's ability to contribute to his team's competitive advantage in growing their joint customer. Which composition of players can best minimize a customer's costs, giving him a competitive edge in becoming his industry's low-cost supplier? Which composition of players can best maximize a customer's revenues and earnings, giving him a competitive edge in becoming his industry's market leader?

Under these terms and conditions of cooperative competition, a poorly partnered business will be noncompetitive because it will not be able to offer the most compelling propositions to other alliances. In turn, once it becomes noncompetitive, it will become progressively unpartnerable.

Positioning in Three Progressive Steps

When you commit yourself to grow as a growth partner, you take on a very different position than committing to grow as a consumer packaged-goods marketer, a power tool manufacturer, or a factory-automation software supplier. If your positioning is based on a product or process, you will lead yourself to believe that something like telecommunications systems or home health-care technology is the source of your growth. When you position yourself as a grower of your customers, you will stop asking "How can we grow?" and start asking "How can we grow our customers?"

Your answers will change your business. If you manufacture computerized laboratory test systems for hospitals, you will ask how you can help your customers' laboratories expand their revenue-generating capability by improving the productivity of their labor forces. If you are a manufacturer of insulation materials for original equipment makers, you will ask how you can help them increase the sales of their products or their margins because your insulation better controls heat. You may also ask how you can reduce their cost of inventorying your materials. Your answers may lead you to partnerships. The more sales your hospital laboratory partners make, the more computerized test systems and consumable products and services you can sell them. The more products your equipment manufacturer partners sell, the more insulation they will need to buy from you.

In order to be positioned to partner in these ways, you must put yourself through three progressive steps. The first step is positioning yourself as a grower in each of your major customer industries. The second step is positioning yourself for growth with each major customer in each major industry. The third step is positioning yourself with each major business-line manager or business-function manager in each major customer.

1. *Industry-specific growth.* You must dedicate your business to be the premier grower in each of your customers' major industries. You must think of yourself as making growth for them, not products or services. You must be experts in their operations and markets, not just your own. You must be their industry standard for controlling the costs of these operations and expanding their profitable sales to these markets.

2. *Customer-specific growth.* You must dedicate your growth capabilities to two types of customers: those who are currently growing because of you and those who are growable by you because their profitability depends on operations whose costs you are expert in reducing or sales whose profitable volume you are expert in expanding.

3. *Manager-specific growth.* You must dedicate your cost reduction and revenue expansion to the two types of managers whose contributions add the most value to their companies'

competitive advantage. One type is your customers' profit center managers who command the lines of business into which your products or services are sold. They must have their contributions to profitable sales volume expanded. The second type is your customers' cost center managers who operate the business functions where your products or services are applied and installed. They must have their contributions to costs reduced.

All customer managers have objectives on which they are graded, compensated, and promoted. In order to position yourself for partnerability with any of them, you must learn their objectives and help them achieve their own personal and professional competitive advantage in relevant categories that may include:

- Annual percentage yield improvement
- Annual percentage cost reduction
- Annual percentage cycle time reduction in design, manufacturing, and order fulfillment
- Annual percentage lead time reduction
- Annual percentage inventory turn increase
- Annual percentage cost reduction for field product failures
- Annual percentage cost reduction for warranty fulfillment, repair, and replacement
- Annual percentage lots accepted to lots produced
- Annual percentage on-time delivery

Partnering by Managing Customer Operations

Over and above reducing the costs and expanding the revenues and earnings that come from supplying products and services to customers, partnering can take a much more managerial stance. Suppliers can approach customers with partnerable propositions like these:

▲ In manufacturing businesses, a supplier can say to a customer, "Let us manage the facility where we have been supplying you. We will make a thorough survey of its growth needs in keeping with the objectives of your strategic plan. We will then recommend the optimal system of products and services to meet your needs. Each product and service will come from the most cost-effective supplier, whether it is us or someone else. We will purchase the system, integrate it, install it, maintain it, upgrade it, and manage its contribution to your profits by means of a three-year business plan. The plan's purpose will be to improve the function's contribution to your profits over what it is currently contributing or could otherwise be expected to contribute. We will guarantee the annual contributions we agree on."

▲ In retailing businesses such as consumer packaged goods, a supplier can say to a retail chain customer: "Let us manage the category where we have been supplying you. We will stock it and shelve it to make the optimal contribution to your profits. We will handle inventory, warehousing and delivery, display, restocking, and promotion. At all times your stores will feature the most profitable mix of competitive products in the category, including ours. We will manage the category according to a continually updated planogram of products together with pricing and promotional support. The planogram's purpose will be to improve the category's contribution to chain profits over what it is currently contributing or could otherwise be expected to contribute. We will guarantee the annual contributions we agree on."

In these relationships as facility manager and category manager, the supplier partner becomes the comanaging partner of a customer operation, function, process, or department. IBM is the facility manager for Kodak's telecommunications functions. Digital Equipment Corporation is the correlate facility manager for Kodak's management information services. Similarly, health care suppliers are partnering with hospital customers to manage their inventories, intensive care units, or home health services. Aircraft manufacturers are partnering with corporate customers to manage their business fleets, supply the optimal mix of pilots, aircraft, and maintenance, and do it all under a management fee that will be less expensive than each customer's former direct cost or more profitable as a generator of revenues.

In order to partner as a customer manager, a supplier must be process-smart about a customer's facility or category and market-smart about his customer's customers. He must also be good at knowing competitive suppliers whose products and services mix optimally with his own. Finally, he must be a good manager so that he can grow a customer's profit contribution by controlling its cost base and extending its base of revenues and earnings.

Partnering as a manager makes a supplier his customer's peer: Both act to manage customer operations, with the supplier acting as an outsource. While the supplier still grows his customers through his products and services, he adds management skills to his growth menu that do more than products or services can ever do to preempt an exclusive partnership. The customer acquires a comanager, a partner in fact as well as in function.

When United Air Lines (UAL) wanted to upgrade its computer system through which its billings and collections flow from travel agencies, Hewlett-Packard Company (HP) proposed to partner with UAL through a joint venture that would operate the airline's travel agency sales.

HP offered to contribute an integrated multivendor computer system, complete with technical and maintenance service support, whose purpose would be to give UAL's travel agents the ability to make more bookings faster.

By improving each agent's transaction turnover and related cash flows, both the agents and the airline would grow.

HP proposed to be the majority owner of the joint venture, holding 81 percent of the voting stock so that the venture could be consolidated on HP's books. UAL would have only a one-line balance sheet entry called "Minority Investment in Joint Venture." Since UAL would not have to disclose any other balance sheet or income statement information, its investment would remain off the airline's books.

HP proposed to finance the lease of its computer systems and services to the joint venture. In turn, the venture would make monthly payments to HP. Correspondingly, the venture would bundle its operating lease payments and charges for services into a single monthly lump sum bill to UAL. The airline would then invoice and collect from its travel agencies and repay the joint venture. Figure 3-1 shows how the venture partners would work together.

In addition to off-balance sheet financing, the operating lease method would allow full monthly payments to be expensed for tax purposes. The lease also offered UAL a purchase option at the end of its four-year term based on 60 percent equity accrual for payments made. At UAL's option, the lease could be renewed beyond four years at a reduced monthly payment.

HP would book an asset in its general ledger as "Investment in UAL Joint Venture" for the amount of its initial investment. This account would be increased annually by HP's 81 percent share of the partnership's net income.

Ensuring a Supply of Managing Partners

Some managers are born partnerable. Most must be made partnerable, homegrown by training in the skills of building someone else's business so that their own business can be grown. Customer-building comes unnaturally to the majority of line managers who are, by nature and design, more likely to be competitive rather than cooperative and self-enhancing rather than partner-enhancing.

The skillset that makes a manager partnerable is a complex of an attitude that says "grow the customer first" and five strategies:

Figure 3-1. HP/UAL joint venture.

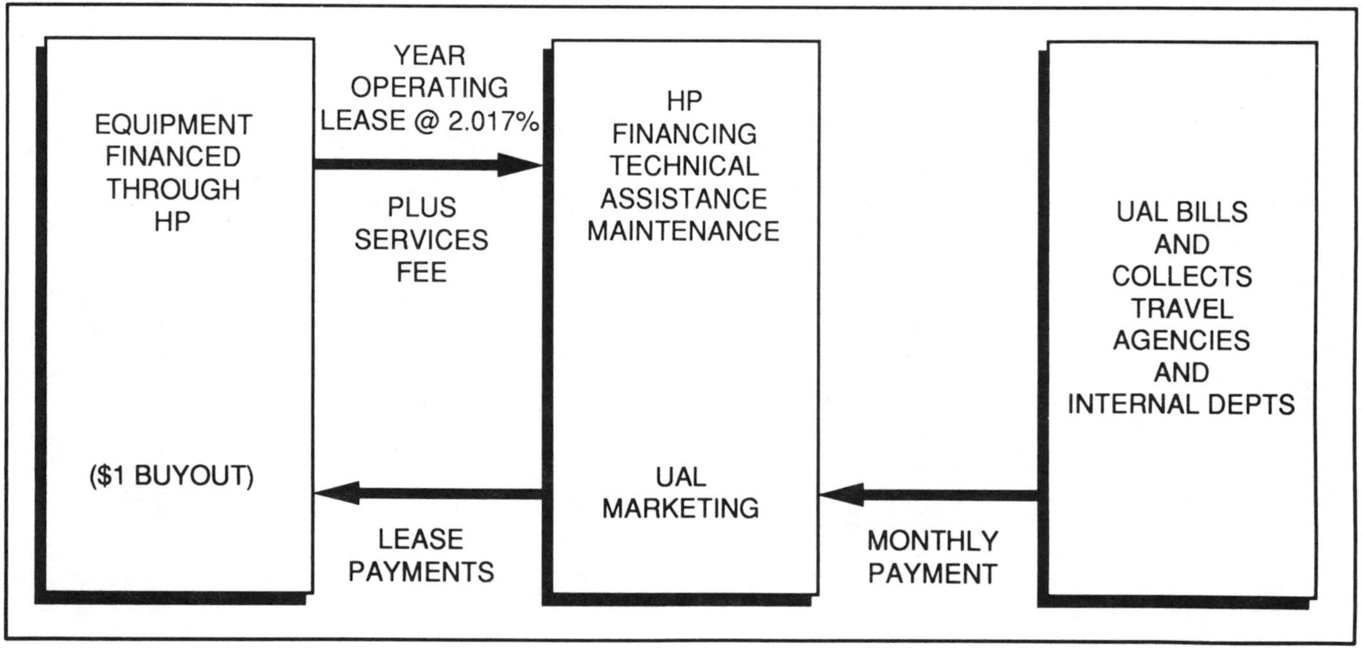

1. *Focus on profit policy.* The number one job of a partnership's growth manager is to manage the partners' mutual rates of return and net profits from each partnered project. The standard of performance is that neither partner's profits can be improved without adding to or subtracting from the project's assets. This ensures that a growth manager is managing for profits, not volume. It also helps warrant that every dollar of the partners' investments will be working cost-effectively, either to keep costs under control or expand the partners' revenues and earnings.

2. *Organize as lean teams.* Profit policy is best implemented through "lean and mean" growth teams that are minimally staffed by both partners to carry out the partnership's profit projects. Each team is resourced according to its mission. Staple components of every team include a financial resource, a data resource, and a technical resource led by the partnership's growth manager.

3. *Practice project management.* Each profit project must be managed like a miniature startup business. It must be planned and operated according to plan to make its numbers at every milestone, and it must follow its critical path to completion on time and on budget.

4. *Concentrate on brand-building.* Growth managers must have a bias for building branded businesses with their partners so that each partnership's products and services will be able to command premium prices. Only differentiable, value-based businesses are worth partnering. Commodity businesses that are already mature may offer cost reduction opportunities by joint venturing to consolidate duplicate asset bases. But even these businesses should be strip-searched for brand potential by adding values to them from application services or consultation.

5. *Adhere to priorities.* Growth managers must focus on three indicators of partnership growth in their standards of performance for each profit project. One is the partners' percentage of profits on sales. The second is their percentage of investment turnover, which measures how well sales are being

used as the drivewheel to maximize the partners' capital circulation. A third indicator is the percentage of assets retrieved from operations if a profit project is based on cost reduction.

The five skills for growth managing replicate the typical skillset of entrepreneurial business ventures. They rivet attention to profits, running lean, staying with priorities, and building high-margin brands. This similarity is purposeful. Partnerships should be treated as business entities. In effect, the partners act as their venture funders. The partnerships they sponsor have only a short time to prove themselves since they must become self-capitalizing quickly and establish a proprietary position in their markets that enables them to stand on their own financial feet.

Growth Teaming in Blue and Gold

Growth partnering is a team game. Instead of playing against each other in the traditionally adversarial buyer-seller relationship, growth teams partner with each other. They combine forces to win against a customer partner's cost problems and to win over other rival partnerships that stand in the way of fully realizing the customer's sales opportunities.

Growth teaming takes place simultaneously on two levels. Each level requires its own leadership style, team composition, and objectives.

Blue Teams for Today's Growth

When partnerships begin, the easiest way for the partners to get started is to work together on a current problem or opportunity where things that are being done right now—or that come around again and again in a predictable cycle—can be done more profitably or more cost-effectively by being done cooperatively. At this level of partnering, immediate payouts can be achieved. This is the Blue Team level for today's growth.

The typical composition of a Blue Team is shown in Figure

3-2. Your customer partner's Blue Team will be its correlate. The teams are deliberate clones, duplicating their four principal resources to provide purposeful overlap of reinforcing skillsets. When Blue Teams come together, they partner on a resource-to-resource basis so that each team represents four subpartnerships reporting to the managerial partnership that drives them.

Blue Teams raise issues like these: What costs that each of their parent companies presently imposes on the other can be reduced? How can they grow each other's current revenues and earnings? What new products, services, or markets can be logically extended from today's mix? What investments can be shared, what support services can be pooled, what technologies paired off, and what additional partners need to be brought in?

Figure 3-2. Blue Team model.

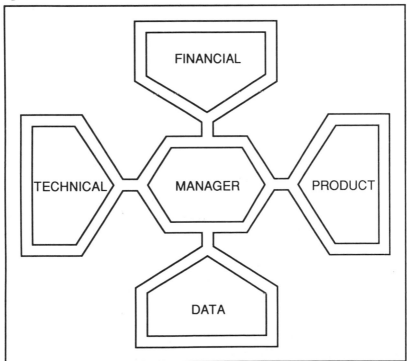

Blue Teams meet in a short-term context. They operate in a tactical theater, making money for the partners that will subsidize the longer term, more strategic mission of the Gold Teams that grow tomorrow's business.

Gold Teams for Tomorrow's Growth

When Gold Teams partner, it is always three years from now. While Blue Teams look downward at today's bottom line, Gold Teams focus their vision upward at tomorrow's top line. What will the future business of the partners be like? Where will their big moneymakers come from? What will their markets be like? Who will their competitors be, what rules are they most likely to play by, and what contributions from each of the partners will be required to play by the new rules and win?

At the Gold Team level, team members must be eclectic. They must be able to think "ahead of the curve," assuming that tomorrow's businesses will not simply be linear extensions of today. Some of them may be more or less radical departures from today that can make current businesses not just noncompetitive but obsolete. This is why Gold Teams are configured as Figure 3-3 shows.

Gold Teams must break new ground. Tomorrow's products and processes, tomorrow's markets, and tomorrow's operating strategies and organization styles are their proper agenda, leaving today's businesses to the Blue Teams. You will have to look for Gold Team members in places like corporate development and in the non-beancounting areas of strategic planning, product and market planning, and market research. Other members can come from R&D and advanced technologies. If you find that you have difficulty fielding men and women for your Gold Teams, you can thank the process of growth partnering for revealing to you, hopefully in time, your unpreparedness for the future.

Rewarding Growth Team Performance

One of the major incentives for partnering should be shared rewards. In order to contribute maximum motivation for the

Figure 3-3. Gold Team model.

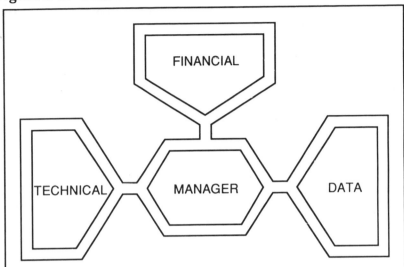

partners to grow each other, rewards for team performance should bookend each profit project. Up-front incentives can be used to encourage intelligent risk-taking at the inception of a partnership. This will evidence itself in setting stretch objectives. Rewards for achievement, for either being on plan or better, serve as proof at the end of each project that its growth risk has been intelligently taken.

A sophisticated reward system should go light on the incentives while heavying up on the rewards. Three types of rewards can be used separately or combined:

1. Progress awards for meeting each planned milestone on budget and on time
2. A final award for being on plan
3. A bonus award for being better than plan

Progress awards are a vital component of growth partner compensation because they are highly motivational. They prove the reward system is working along with the partnership. They also emphasize the time value of growth. Missing a milestone incurs a calculable opportunity cost. It may also jeopardize the entire project. Its opportunity window may be foreshortened, transforming its planned longevity into unplanned "shortgevity."

There are three key milestones in the life cycle of every profit project where progress rewards should cluster: *market entry*, the point where a partnership goes commercial; *breakeven*, the point where the partners' investment achieves payback; and *accelerated growth*, the point where the planned rate of accelerated growth kicks in.

There are two rules to remember in setting up a partnered reward schedule. One is that each growth team should be compensated based on the profits it improves for its partner or, if the partnership is a joint business entity, for the co-owned corporation. The second rule is that the compensation schedule should be unfair. It should be prejudiced in favor of disproportionately rewarding growth managers and their teams rather than their companies.

A model reward schedule contains four elements: a performance bonus, profit sharing, real or phantom equity, and a cafeteria of supplementary awards.

1. *Bonus on base salary.* For managers and their growth teams, a bonus up to 50 percent of base salary to a total of 10 times salary if 100 percent of a project's planned objectives are met on time.

2. *Profit share.* An additional 20 percent share of each project's net profits after taxes.

3. *Equity.* An additional 20 percent ownership stake in phantom shares, or real shares if the partnership is a third-party corporation, valued at 5 to 10 times earnings with a call on 10 to 15 percent more.

4. *Cafeteria of supplementary awards.* A menu of other benefits can be included in a cafeteria-style reward schedule. Common to many of them is a deferred option up to 100 percent payable in 25 percent increments:

- ▲ Joint "Chairman's Awards" of $10,000 from each partnering company.
- ▲ A bank of growth units, a form of scrip, which are assigned a negative value at the inception of a profit project, increase to zero value on the planned realization of cost savings or new product commercialization, and progress to be worth successively higher values as the partnership grows.

As a corrolary to the award of growth units, up to 20 percent of them may be vested following a project's realization at an assigned value per unit. Once banked, their value will rise or fall with the project's success. If a growth milestone is missed, the teams will suffer a commensurate withdrawal from their bank accounts.

Partnering at the Top

Partnering at the top, by one chief executive with another, is becoming one of the most important moneymaking functions of partnering. It is the one function that cannot be delegated. Major sales, where multiple millions of dollars hang in the balance for both companies, must increasingly be made by the two top managers who alone can commit their total resources and enforce their implementation.

Chief officers are the sole managers who possess the overview skills, backed by their corporate credibility, to be able to predict the economic impact that the capabilities of one company can make on the operations and their contrition to profits of another.

Top managers partnering in this way are actually performing mutual money-management function. They are ensuring the creation of critical incremental values in the businesses of their major suppliers and customers. In turn, they are reensuring critical values of their own. In order to perform as the ultimate partner of their businesses, tomorrow's men and women at the top will have to know two sets of facts by heart:

1. Where a partner's cost problems that they can affect are clustered, how to affect them so that they can be substantially reduced or eliminated, and how to quantify the improved economic and production values that can result.
2. Where a partner's market opportunities that they can affect are located, how to affect them so that they can be more fully realized, and how to quantify the values in improved competitive advantage that can result.

Top-level partnering is the supreme match-up of one partner's capabilities with another partner's needs, both for the present and the future. "Where are you planning to take your business this coming year?" is each president's opening question to initiate the annual relationship. The follow-on question becomes, "Where are you planning to take your business over the next three to five years?"

The need-seeking and capability-matching that emerge from joint planning at the top give each chief officer insight into what he can expect or expect to have from the other: What needs does the customer partner have that the supplier partner can fill? What capabilities does the supplier partner have or require that the customer partner can benefit from?

What will supplier-company presidents be looking for in this process of mutual discovery? They must learn things like this from their customers: What new businesses are you planning to venture into? What markets will they serve? What new requirements will that introduce into your business—for new or enhanced products, manufacturing processes, information technology, or sales and distribution systems? What new competitive advantages in cost control or productivity will you require in order to be able to fulfill your growth plans?

What growth businesses are you counting on to provide the bulk of your new profits? What do they require to maintain or improve their current rates of growth? What constraints must they overcome that can get in the way of achieving their objectives?

Which of your heavy revenue generators, the shooting

stars and cash cows in your company, do you plan to fund more generously in order to keep them competitive? Will you allocate these funds to reduce their costs or increase their revenues or market share? Which of your declining businesses do you plan to turn around? Which do you plan to divest? Are any of them likely to become leveraged buyouts?

Each answer represents a potential partnered business opportunity. Based on these answers, a supplier can plan his capabilities mix, allocate a proper proportion of it to each major customer's needs, and target the opportunities to sell them at the correct entry points in each customer company. The supplier knows when and where his customer's funds are going to flow. This tells him which business units will be fed or starved; which will have budgets and can buy based on value; and which will be able to buy, if at all, only on price. It also tells him where to partner based on cost reduction and where a sales revenue increase for a customer will be the compelling partnerable appeal. Finally, it gives him an idea of how much profit he can expect to earn from each customer partnership.

A customer learns the contribution that he can expect from each supplier. What can he count on in terms of quality, innovation, delivery, and value-to-price? Can he ally with a particular supplier as a sole source? Is the supplier a better cost-reducer than revenue-increaser? How much incremental profits can be expect from each supplier and when can he expect it?

Partnerships at the top levels will be based on an exchange of profits. For the customer, keeping his major suppliers profitable is essential to his continued access to the capabilities he needs for his growth. For the supplier, the customer is the source of his growth funds. Without profitable customers whose earnings are growing at a rapid, sustained rate, the only prospect will be for no growth or slow growth.

Each member of a partnership has the same responsibility: grow the other. There is no better place to set the drive force for a grow-grow relationship than at the top where the power to manage growth, as well as its responsibility, are concentrated.

4

Prospecting for Growth Partners

Partnering is the net result of two choices. The first choice is your selection of customers to grow. The second choice is made by your customers. Why should they select you?

Your partnerability requires more than a reputation for quality products, professional management people, or a similarity of corporate cultures. It would be difficult to pair off two companies that meet these criteria more fully than Hewlett-Packard and Northern Telecom. Yet their alliance to sell integrated computer and telecommunications networks was almost totally unproductive. Their technical strengths and conservative cultures reinforced each other while their mutual weaknesses in strategic planning, market knowledge, and Consultative Selling were similarly compounded.

Other partnerships fail because the partners multiply each other's differences, such as one company's entrepreneurialism creating unaffordable costs of friction by chafing against an ally's bureaucratic management style.

Your partnerability with any one of your natural partners will be situational as well as cultural, depending on a combination of rightness of fit and timeliness. It will also be relative rather than absolute. There are no ideal mates. When you assess your partnerability, you should analyze your business vis-à-vis each individual candidate for partnership according to a handful of standards:

▲ Does the situation call for overlapping strengths or does it require each of us to be strong where the other is weak? Do we have the right "strength mix?"

▲ Are we similar enough in wanting to grow to get along? Does each of us have a growth culture regardless of any other cultural attributes?

▲ Will we be an important source of growth profits? Will we be able to deliver them in timely fashion, recognizing the time value of our partner's money and his susceptibility to opportunity cost? Will we be a dependable profitmaker for him?

▲ Will we be a preferred triple-A blue chip investment, offering our partner a better place for his money than any other partnership or a comparable investment in his own business?

▲ Will we have the same competitors—which is another way of asking if we have mutual objectives—in the form of costs that affect both of us that must be reduced or revenues that can give both of us a competitive advantage if they are expanded?

You may also need a new positioning. In order to maximize your partnerability, you will have to think and act like a partner. This means that you will have to transform the vision you hold of your business from being a supplier of products and services to a supplier of profits. This will convert you from representing an added cost to an added value.

Positioning yourself as a value-adding partner takes practice. It means thinking reflexively of what may be in it for your partner as soon as you suspect that there may be something significant in it for yourself. As an example, suppose that you can envision a value in adding the rights to distribute another company's product line to your current market. You should train yourself to calculate almost simultaneously the potential value to your partner of adding the value of your sales and distribution capabilities to his marketing mix. This is the value you will have to sell when you propose a growth partnership. Instead of saying that you would like to add his products to your line, say, "What if you can add 250 field salespeople calling on 1,000 prospective customers each day—beginning at once— without having to hire a single one of them or cultivate a single one of their customers: How much can that add to your revenues and earnings over the next twelve months?"

Certifying Your Growth Partners

If you are going to grow, you must be a grower so that the partners you grow can maximize your growth in return. Being a grower means that you know who you can grow best, fastest, and surest. It means knowing how much you can most likely grow them and how soon your growth contributions can flow to fund their objectives. It means being sure. It also means the converse of all these things: you know how much your partners can grow you in return, how fast, and how sure.

No matter what business you are in, you have customers who are natural growth partners. They are businesses whose growth is interdependent with yours. In one or more significant ways, their growth depends on you and your growth depends on them. The most important decision in managing your business is to certify who your natural growth partners are.

If you are a going concern, you have two types of growth partners. One is the customers you are already growing. The other is the customers who are growable by you but you are not yet growing. A startup business has all its customers in the second category.

The act of 80-20ing an up-and-running business reveals who its current growth partners are. They will be the 20 percent or fewer of all its customers who are contributing up to 80 percent or more of its profitable sales volume. They are already growing their suppliers because their suppliers are already growing them by delivering value that is adding to their competitive advantage.

The customers that you are already growing are more than your greatest current growth source. They are also your greatest potential growth source. Your two businesses have already proved that you have a natural ability to grow each other. This suggests that you can grow each other even more. Furthermore, you already know some important facts about their businesses. This gives you a base for learning even more, especially since you know who their main managers are who can give you the access you require to offer them a partnerable proposition.

Your second greatest growth source is composed of your growable prospects. These are companies that have similar cost problems or revenue opportunities to the customers you are already growing. Their cost-centered business functions will be familiar to you. So will their profit-centered lines of business.

You should ask three questions about both your current growth customers and your growable prospects to start your selection process.

Current customers

1. How are we growing them right now?
2. How much are we growing them compared to how much they are growing us?
3. How much more can we grow them and be grown by them?

Growable prospects

1. How can we grow them?
2. How much can we grow them compared to how much they can grow us?
3. What new capabilities must we invest in so that we can grow them?

Within the mix of the customers you are currently growing and your growable customers, you should look for three general indicators of prime partnerability:

1. *Nascent opportunity.* A customer that is undergoing rapid growth or is reorganizing, restructuring, or rightsizing for renewed growth is an enhanced partnership candidate. Change at the top is an added enhancement, putting new managers in

power who may be especially receptive to the competitive advantages of alliance.

2. *Positive attitude.* A customer who prefers to partner makes the best partner. Receptivity to your partnering proposition will be ensured and so will a heightened interest in controlling costs and expanding revenues and earnings through allying.

3. *Marketable repute.* A sophisticated customer with a reputation for running a good business at high standards of performance will have some of the best managers to partner with. They will be able to maximize your contributions, increasing your odds for success and your ability to come away with a reference for your partnerability that will attract similarly sophisticated partners to you.

Figures 4-1 and 4-2 are a related set of partnerability grids. They allow you to calculate the most likely contributions you can make to candidates for partnership with you, both in cost reduction and revenue expansion. Figures 4-3 and 4-4 represent a reciprocal set of partnerability grids. They allow you to calculate the most likely contributions each candidate can make to you. A candidate with whom you can give and receive competitive advantage that is significant to each of you is an incipient growth partner.

The business planning of every partnership you enter should begin with partnerability grids. Page one of every business plan should identify your growth partners, since they—not a process or product or service or system—will be the true sources of your prosperity and therefore the origins of your business opportunity. Businesses originate in markets, not technologies. Managers who allege in their plans that they "have a business here" should be required to prove it by their ability to certify the customer businesses that they can grow that can grow them back. *The proof of a business opportunity is not a commercializable science but partnerable customers.*

If you know who your natural growth partners are and what they need from you in order to grow, you can dedicate

(Text continued on page 56.)

Figure 4-1. Partnerability grid: cost reduction to a partner.

	Most Likely Contribution to Their Cost Reduction ($000)	*Most Likely Time Frame to Achieve (mos/yrs)*	*Most Likely Strategy to Partner*
Candidate A _____	_____	_____	
Candidate B _____	_____	_____	
Candidate C _____	_____	_____	

Figure 4-2. Partnerability grid: revenue expansion to a partner.

	Most Likely Contribution to Their Revenue Expansion ($000)	*Most Likely Time Frame to Achieve (mos/yrs)*	*Most Likely Strategy to Partner*
Candidate A _____	_____	_____	
Candidate B _____	_____	_____	
Candidate C _____	_____	_____	

Figure 4-3. Partnerability grid: cost reduction from a partner.

	Most Likely Contribution to Our Cost Reduction ($000)	*Most Likely Time Frame to Achieve (mos/yrs)*	*Most Likely Strategy to Partner*
Candidate A	_____	_____	
Candidate B	_____	_____	
Candidate C	_____	_____	

Figure 4-4. Partnerability grid: revenue expansion from a partner.

	Most Likely Contribution to Our Revenue Expansion ($000)	*Most Likely Time Frame to Achieve (mos/yrs)*	*Most Likely Strategy to Partner*
Candidate A	_____	_____	
Candidate B	_____	_____	
Candidate C	_____	_____	

your business to them from the outset. Your business can be structured as a reciprocal of their needs for accelerated growth. Your capabilities can be responses to their needs, your profit centers can have a one-to-one relationship with their lines of business that you will grow, and your data bases can contain knowledge of their growth constraints and opportunities.

Taking the First Steps

To try to start a partnership by saying to a customer or supplier "We want to partner with you" is to say nothing. This is a getting-to-lunch statement instead of getting to work.

The easiest way to start, which means going operational with a partner, is by asking two questions at the initiative of either the customer or supplier:

1. *What costs can be reduced in their business with us?* Which costs are the 20 percent that make up 80 percent of their total costs of doing business with us? (To be asked by both suppliers and customers about each other.)
   a. How much are the costs?
   b. How do they compare with costs of doing business with competitive suppliers or customers:
      —Where are we costliest to them?
      —By how much?
      —Where are we least costly to them?
      —By how much?
   c. Which of these categories of cost are on their "must list" to reduce?
   d. What actions can we take?
2. *What revenues and earnings can be expanded in their business with us?* Which of our products and services are the 20 percent that give them 80 percent of their total revenues and earnings from doing business with us? (To be asked by suppliers about their business with customers.)
   a. How much are their revenues in our categories?
   b. How much are their margins?

      c. How do they compare with revenues and margins from competitive suppliers:
- —Where are we their volume leader?
- —By how much?
- —Where are we their profit leader?
- —By how much?
- —Where are we least profitable to them?
- —By how much?

      d. Which of these business categories are on their "must list" to expand?

      e. What actions can we take?

In each of these areas of inquiry, partners ask what they can do for each other:

Which of *your costs* that you are incurring in working with us can we help you reduce? Which of *your revenue streams* that are contributed by our products and services can we help you expand?

Where do we cost you the most; how can we reduce it? Where do we make the least money for you; how can we expand it? How can we expand even the categories where we are already making the most money for you?

Which of our current categories of business are among your growth priorities? What new categories of business—products, services, distribution strategies—are among your growth priorities and how can we jointly maximize their contributions? How will you be organized around these new categories; how can we create a partnered organization structure that can fit hand-in-glove with your own? What should we both be doing to integrate our information technology to link together these new operations on a real-time basis?

What types of people will staff your new operations? Who do we need on our side to be able to relate to them as partners? What background should they have—what traits and characteristics as well as skills?

The decision to work as partners requires that three conditions be met:

1. The prospective profits from growing a customer should exceed the current costs or opportunity losses from the customer's problem. This ensures that partnered growth will be more profitable than not growing as partners.
2. The prospective profits from growing a customer should exceed the prospective costs of growth. This ensures that the partnership's rate of return on the investment to grow will be positive.
3. The prospective profits from growing a customer should exceed the prospective profits from doing something else. This ensures that the partners' opportunity cost is minimized.

All customer businesses and business functions can be thought of as a "mix." Some mixes make products or provide services. Other mixes sell them. Still other mixes support the sales mix through aftersale services such as training, applications, and maintenance. You have partnering opportunity in any mix whose composition you can optimize: that is, where you can contribute a significant reduction in the cost of the mix or a significant expansion of its contribution to revenues and earnings. Every mix that you can optimize becomes a growth partnering opportunity. If you can optimize a mix better than any other supplier, you can position yourself as its mixmaster.

Customer mixes usually lag behind an optimal mix. They frequently represent a sizable investment. They also are tied to a customer's learning curve. The customer's people have learned how to operate their current mix and are familiar with its capabilities and its quirks. Training programs have been built around it. Cost and production schedules are established for it. Culturally, it has become "the way we do things around here." It must be approached remedially but respectfully. You do not want to run a customer's businesses. You want to partner with a customer's managers so that they *can run the businesses better.*

There are three strategies for optimizing any customer:

1. Supplant one or more elements in the current mix. If the mix is labor intensive, reduce labor content by substituting an automated process or eliminating an operation altogether. Combine multiple processes in a customer's sales function, such as forecasting and inventory control, thereby eliminating overlapping and duplicated costs.

2. Substitute your product or process for a competitive product or process that is part of the customer's current mix. The basis for your proposal must be that improved financial benefits will accrue to the customer if the mix is altered and not simply that more advantageous performance benefits will be realized.

3. Restructure or manage the mix in a newly significant manner. In addition to the improvement in profits from becoming your partner, the prestige of working with you as the leading mix integrator or facility manager may provide extra motivation for customers to partner with you.

In order to make mix optimizing work, each partner must be obsessed with his partner's growth and the contribution he must make to it. Questions such as these must predominate in each partner's mindset:

1. How can I grow my partner more today?
2. How can I grow him even more tomorrow?

It takes forbearance to put your partner first, transcending the natural reflexes of managing your business. Growth partnering is a conditioned reflex, a learned response to the realization that your business cannot grow itself; that only your customers and suppliers can grow you. If you want to be a partner, you will have to condition yourself to growing someone else's business before your own business can be grown. The answer to "How can we grow?" is always found in the question "How can we grow our partners?"

Whenever growth is being planned, you must think of your partner first. How will this strategy grow him? Will it grow him enough? Will it grow him fast enough? How sure will his growth be? Is this the best strategy to grow him? If not, it will not be the best strategy to grow your business either.

Organizing Around Your Partners

Customer partners must be recognized for the central role they play in your growth. The way you recognize them should be two-fold: first, in the type of managers you assign to grow them, in the joint teams you staff, and in the growth planning process you share with your partners; and second, in the way you organize your business for partnering.

Traditional organization structures, whether they are functionally based on a process or product-based, resist partnering. They operate from a physical asset base rather than a customer asset base. They are designed to sell products or services rather than customer growth. They focus on their own competitors instead of your customers and your customers' competitors, making it their mission to deny growth to your competition rather than accelerate growth for your customers.

A growth organization, structured from a standing start to grow customers, starts with your customers as the focal point of its form and substance and grows your business around them. Growable customers are at its center. A customer-centered organization is customer derived, customer oriented, and customer specific from its inception.

Figure 4-5 shows a model growth center. Its manager is in charge of three functions: development, sales, and financial control. The growth center manager acts as a prime contractor, obtaining the internal and externally outsourced capabilities that he or she needs to fulfill the center's growth plans with each customer partner. As such, each growth center can be thought of as a growth club.

Under this type of management structure, three traditional business functions disappear. R&D and marketing vanish as in-

Figure 4-5. Model growth center.

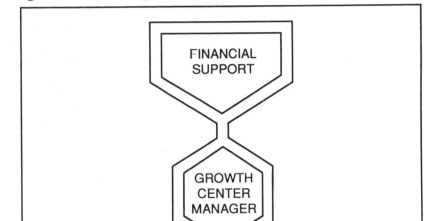

dependent entities, becoming a single development function. The general sales manager function disappears along with them but reappears in the form of two managers instead of one: a manager of partnered sales and a manager of vended sales.

1. *Development management.* The development function combines the normally separate processes of technical development with the sales development activities of marketing. It is responsible for generating a continuing succession of new business opportunities of superior profit potential that can command premium unit margins as their basis for growth.

2. *Sales management.* The sales function is divided into two salesforces. One salesforce vends commodity products to purchasing and technical-buying engineering managers based on price/performance values. The second salesforce sells branded products, services, and systems at premium margins to top-tier customer decision makers who control business functions or who run business units. The growth center manager is responsible for planning the optimal mix of these two salesforces so that the center's profit and volume objectives are cost-effectively achieved.

3. *Financial support.* The development function and the top-tier sales function both require guidance on how each can best maximize customer profits. Financial support services help the development function manager calculate the customer profit values that must be delivered by each product's performance benefits before they are engineered. Financial support also helps top-tier sales management calculate value-based prices based on the profit values that can be delivered to customers as a result of partnering.

In a growth center, customer needs seed product development. They inspire development, set its boundaries, and are inextricably incorporated into its creations. Otherwise development can never be tuned to the real world of its market. Nor will marketing be anything more than an exercise in the control of unsold inventory, price discounting, and closeouts.

As long as they remain separate functions, marketing and research are strangers at best. At worst they are adversaries. R&D invents the inventable, but not necessarily the marketable. Researchers, cut off from the market, work to impress their peers or amaze their competitors. Marketers, whose eye may be more on competition than on customers, typically respond by ordering products with ever-increasing performance benefits. Whether or not they achieve a momentary superiority, they invariably cause overengineering and its consequent overcosting. Even though the products that emerge from this process may work better than anything on the market, their cost-ineffectiveness makes it impossible for them to sell at growth profits.

Joining R&D and marketing into a combined customer developer organization brings them and their customers together organizationally in a common cause. Each now has the customer as master. Who controls whom is predetermined. The customer rules, both as a participating partner and through representation in the data bases around which the customer development function is organized.

The marketing-R&D data base is a growth supplier's shrine. It replaces parochial places of worship such as the vat, the hearth, or the mold. Foremost among the data are the quantified needs of partnered customers for improvement in their profits and productivity. They become the development function's directives. Build to them, inventors are told. Price according to the value of the solution you can offer, marketers are charged.

Performance values—the physical, chemical, and electronic features that historically preoccupy R&D and frequently mesmerize marketers—assume their proper role as contributors to customer profits. But they are no longer business objectives in themselves. How much customer profit will they contribute? How soon? How sure? Unless customer profit objectives are met, a product cannot be said to "work" for a partnership no matter how impressive its technical credentials or performance achievements.

When customers are brought into the development process from day one, it is unnecessary to market its results. The market is already engineered into each product. Development has become a customer-dedicated process through which user needs have been internalized.

Marketing as a separate organization function is surplus for a partnered growth center. A structural partnership between marketing and R&D demonstrates that a growth partner, like his customers, cares not at all whether the inspiration for new customer values originates in the minds of marketers or developers. Released from rivalry between the two functions, you can focus on the most significant sources of new customer values. These are rarely product values. More likely they will be the values of application, installation, education, consultation,

Figure 4-6. Growth network.

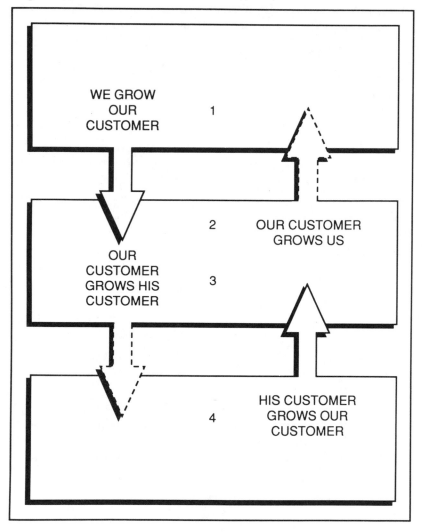

and documentation of the improved customer profits that a product initiates but, in and of itself, can never fulfill.

By organizing a growth center for each of your major customer markets, you have the opportunity to create a tripartite growth network in each industry composed of you and your allied suppliers in your growth center, its customer partners, and their customer partners. Within each network, each member can participate in the growth of all the other members.

As Figure 4-6 shows, a growth network begins when you and your allies grow a customer. This is step one in the figure. In step two, the customer grows you in return, creating a growth cell. In steps three and four, the customer grows one of his own customers and the customer grows him, creating a second growth cell. Through progressive partnering, the network can continue to proliferate as more growth cells are honeycombed with it.

5

Planning a
Growth Partnership

Partnered growth requires partnered plans for growth. Planning in private, planning from only your own resources, planning against your competitors instead of planning to make your customers more competitive are strategies of growth by conquest instead of growth by collaboration.

Once you have chosen your current customers to grow and the prospectively growable customers you want to add to your partnerships, you are ready to make growth planning a joint enterprise. There are four rules to keep in mind for partnered planning that differ from the traditional formula for strategic business plans:

1. *Set mutually agreeable objectives.* Partners partner around their partnership's objectives. The partnership's joint goals become their individual goals; in turn, individual goals become subsets of the partnership's goals. The joint goals of partners are always supreme. If one partner's rewards are achieved but the partnership's goals as a whole remain unmet, the partnership will be at imminent risk.

2. *Create mutually participative strategies.* Each partner must have his part to play, and must play his part, in achieving the partnership's objectives. Performance must be based on self-starting initiative. Communication must be wide open, with no hidden agendas. Early warning signals of impending perform-

ance failures must be made known in time to correct their problems. It is an ironclad rule that there must be no surprises based on assumptions or "I-thought-you-knews."

3. *Make mutually validated measurements.* A partnership's achievements must be measured jointly while they are in progress so that on-line corrections can be made as soon as deviations from plan are detected. As the partnership's first product, the measurement system must be agreed to before the partnership starts its business. It must stay in place for as long as the partnership endures.

4. *Prepare a partnered profit plan.* A plan committing the partners to their mutual objectives, strategies, and measurement method must become the partners' bible. It should contain the partnership's statement of mission, its pro forma cash flow projections over the first three years of the partnership, and a data base on the partnered products and services or processes and their customers. Page one of the plan must stipulate the dollar values that each partner plans to contribute to the growth of the other, along the lines of Figures 4-1 through 4-4.

Basing Objectives on ROI

There are two prime partnership objectives. The first is *minimum acceptable return on investment (ROI) before taxes,* which runs upward from 10 percent higher than ROI after taxes. The second is *minimum annual net profit before taxes,* which may be twice or more the aftertax profit. Each of these objectives must be expressed within a time frame for its accomplishment. All other objectives are supportive. A model statement of a growth partnership's objectives, constructed in narrative form to show how it might be recited as a commitment to prime and supportive objectives, is shown in Figure 5-1.

ROI and growth profit objectives are planned as the beneficiaries of several supportive objectives such as sales unit and dollar volume, rate of annual sales growth, percentage share of market, and total marketing investment.

Figure 5-1. Statement of objectives.

> The minimum objectives of the partnership are to yield an annual pretax return on investment of 30 percent over a projected three-year growth phase of the partnership's life cycle, together with a $5 million cumulative profit before taxes by Year Five, representing a 30 percent net profit before taxes.
>
> These objectives will be achieved by generating annual net retail sales at the rate of $25 million commencing in Year One from a minimum of three product and service systems, each with a projected minimum annual growth rate of 8 percent, based on a minimum 20 percent share of market.

Figure 5-2. Partnership ROI.

Profit margin expressed as return on sales	Return on capital expressed as capital turnover

$$\text{ROI} = \frac{\text{net operating profit expressed as income from earnings}}{\text{sales}} \times \frac{\text{sales}}{\text{total investment in capital assets employed}}$$

Return on investment relates a partnership's expected profit to the investment risked to earn it. The basic ROI formula defines profit as the rate of profit on sales or operating profit as a percentage of sales. Investment is defined as the total capital assets employed to produce sales. As Figure 5-2 shows, ROI compares profit margin with asset turnover: that is, a partnership's earnings in terms of gross sales income and the capital assets employed to generate them.

Dealing With the ROI Variables

ROI is generally the best way of expressing the yield on total capital employed in a partnership, both human and nonhuman. It can be *determined* by comparing predicted profit with investment. But to understand how ROI can be *managed*, partners must be skilled in dealing with each of the two independent variables that contribute to profit and investment.

The first variable component of ROI, the profit margin expressed as the return on sales, is affected by all the elements included in the total cost of sales—sales volume, price, product mix, factory costs, marketing and administrative expenses, and any other factor affecting profit on sales.

Profit on sales is only one-half of the ROI equation. The management of capital turnover is equally important. A 20 percent profit margin multiplied by a capital turnover rate of one yields a 20 percent ROI. But a 10 percent profit margin can yield a 20 percent ROI when multiplied by a capital turnover rate of two. This second component of ROI, the investment base, is affected by the movement of assets such as inventory levels, turnover of accounts receivable, and plant and equipment expenditures: in short, all the factors that compose investment or affect its rate of turnover as related to sales. A partnership's investment base is considered to be optimal when improvements in net profit are no longer possible by adding to or subtracting from the base.

Since either of the two ROI components may be managed independently of each other, ROI can be improved by two types of strategy:

1. Maximize the profit margin or sales without disproportionately decreasing investment turnover through charging higher prices for the volume of goods sold or through selling a higher volume of goods.
2. Reduce the investment in capital employed without disproportionately increasing the cost of sales through

lowering inventories, speeding the collection of accounts receivable, and limiting additions to property owned by the partners.

Each of the three components interrelated by the basic ROI formula—profit, sales, and investment—has a precise meaning within the ROI context. *Sales* refers to sales income, or net sales as billed. *Profit* represents the supply of assets. *Investment* is the demand on assets.

Partnership profit is net profit, the residual income from profit multiplied by turnover after deduction of operating costs and expenses. Since profit represents the usable earnings on investment, it can be thought of as the manager's wage rate for the risk of capital. For most purposes of computing ROI, profit is usually net profit after taxes, or NPAT.

Partnership investment is the sum total of all capital assets employed to generate profit, figured at net book value. "Total assets" means more than just "invested capital" or "capital employed." It includes all the fixed, variable, and combination of fixed-variable investments that contribute to profit: money, people, projects, and property.

Fixed investments are costs that do not change as the volume of production or sales changes within existing plant and equipment capacity. General and administrative expenses are fixed investments. So is property in the form of land, buildings, machinery, furniture and equipment, rents and taxes on such property, its insurance and depreciation costs, and basic light, heat, power, and communications utilities.

Variable investments are costs that change in direct proportion to changes in volume of production or sales. Selling expenses such as sales commissions and travel and entertainment expenses are variable investments, as are materials and noncontractual labor costs.

Combined fixed-variable investments are costs that change randomly with changes in volume of production or sales. Advertising and sales promotion expenses are combined fixed-variable investments.

Establishing the Three ROI Guidelines

ROI guidelines are basic criteria for determining the businesses a partnership will choose to enter. Once in, the partners can then use these guidelines to help maximize the profitability of each business:

1. The *appraisal guideline* of evaluating current performance, which may be phrased in the question, "Given an $80,000 yield on $500,000 worth of invested assets in business A, for a return on investment of 16 percent, how can the management of these assets be judged?"

2. The *predictive guideline* of forecasting future performance, which may be phrased in the question, "Given an increase of $250,000 worth of invested assets in business B, what return on investment can be forecast by the manager of these assets?"

3. The *incentive guideline* of motivating current and future performance, which may be phrased in the question, "Given the objective of a 16 percent return on a $500,000 investment, what incentive will maximize the manager's certainty of achieving or exceeding this objective?"

ROI as an appraisal guideline. Achievement of the ROI objective is the ultimate measure of a partnership's management. It allows current profit performance to be compared with its planned target. On a this year/last year basis, the managing partners' current performance can be compared with past performance in similar businesses. Within each market segment, the performance of one mix of assets can be compared with others.

ROI as a predictive guideline. The ROI objective helps forecast strategy. Will ROI be enhanced if the capitalization of the partnership's mix is increased? If so, by how much? The partners can forecast the need for incremental investment. Will ROI be enhanced if the product or service components of the mix are altered? If so, the partners can forecast an altered product and service system mix. Will ROI be enhanced if the promotion components of the mix are altered in the form of advertising and sales promotion or in the form of the compensation, motivation, or distribution of the sales force? If so, the partners can forecast an altered promotion mix.

ROI as an incentive guideline. Partnership managers merit unusual reward when they exceed their objectives. When rate of return on investment is used as a prime objective, money or equity incentives can be pegged to each percentage point of ROI overachievement up to the point at which incentive will be maximized.

Living With Limits on ROI

When ROI is used as the primary objective for a partnered business, it may encourage short-term planning and cause managers to overlook opportunities with longer term but greater payoffs. Some partners may believe that a more acceptable objective is a manager's ability to optimize performance rather than generate superior profits. Other partners may feel that ROI is a limited objective because of the difficulty in setting equitable profit objectives for a new business.

Another factor that may reduce the reliability of ROI as an objective is that a partnership is originally top-heavy with new investment. In fact, a newly partnered business may be nothing but a sunk cost for as much as a twelve to eighteen month period: a cost center that yields nothing but negative cash flows. ROI may therefore be less than the best reflection of short-term to medium-term management performance. At the same time and for the same reason, it may also be less than a sufficiently exact instrument for financial control.

A new partnership's objectives can rarely be set with an accuracy common to ongoing businesses. In addition, profit measurements are bound to be inexact because operating conditions in a new enterprise will always vary more or less widely from going-in assumptions. As a result, managers often define ROI according to the real world of their situation. Instead of fixing a minimum ROI, they set a lower ROI objective when the risk appears greater and a higher ROI objective when the results seem more certain or when a partnership's investment will be measurably benefitted by an established business. By doing this, they are setting their expectations of a rate of return at a realistic level commensurate with the degree of difficulty of their business and the length of the time frame over which it can be expected to mature.

The partnership's investment base is more than just the denominator in the ROI formula. It is the planning base as well. It is hoped that every cost will help yield increased profitable sales. But sales can be increased without increasing income. In this simple fact lies the managerial dilemma of the long-range versus the short-range strategy of partnership management.

If partners play the game for the short run, many variable discretionary costs can be eliminated or reduced. Without adding to sales, the partners can produce increased profits by controlling the magnitude of their investment. There are many cost-reducing temptations. Sales force compensation and motivation investments can be postponed. Advertising can be cut back or cycled in periodic waves rather than directed continuously against a market. Second generation new product development may be temporized. Instead, marginal renovations of the partners' original product line may be made to suffice. New plant and equipment investments may be put off.

The more successful these short-range strategies prove themselves to be in constraining costs, the greater the danger that they may also produce considerable long-range cost to the partners' competitive position. Although current profits may be immediately enhanced, three-year profits may be adversely, perhaps fatally, affected as the initial impact of the partnership peters out, plant and equipment age and incur eventually increasing costs, and marketing momentum slows.

On the other hand, there are equal temptations to play the game for the long run. Substantial immediate costs incurred for speculative future profits will immediately penalize short-range earnings. But because they do so in the guise of planning ahead, a manager's escape from the requirement to produce current profits may go unnoticed or at least unsuspected. While the manager is "building for the future," the present can often be sacrificed so severely that the future is compromised before it arrives.

It is easy to say that the optimal course is therefore midway between the temptation to spend less in the short range and more for the long range. Such a middle course might average out failure but it could also average out success. As a result, it might be the strategy of greatest risk.

Partners must appreciate that there can be low-investment years when the short-range game can be played profitably with safety. There is also a corresponding need for high-investment years to seed the next cycle of opportunity. Nor must years necessarily be the basic unit of a partnership's cost accounting. Costs may be allocated against the life cycle of a market need rather than a rounded-off unit of calendar months. Regardless of the basic unit of reckoning, the partners must be more deeply concerned with the rate of return's trend over a three-year period than with the absolute rate of return at any given time. It is on this ongoing basis that the partners must plan.

Any year can be a low-yield year because of deliberately incurred investment costs. Similarly, any year can be a high-yield year because of deliberately reduced or postponed investment costs. It is the trend that matters, so much so that a partnered business may be said to be operating optimally when, over each three-year cycle, its profit yield could not have increased by adding to or subtracting from its investment base.

ROI concentration may also impose too narrow a framework on business selection. Simply because an opportunity to partner promises to yield less than a required ROI may not, in and of itself, be sufficient reason to pass it by. The experience of DuPont when a 20 percent minimum rate of return was a standard objective is worth remembering. While the minimum was in force, the company passed up Xerography and the Land Polaroid camera. In these instances, emphasis on ROI provided a microview of opportunity rather than a macroview.

Creating Growth Strategies

All growth strategies are not created equal. Some are more profitable than others; some of the others are more cost-effective than profitable.

As Figure 5-3 shows, the two principal strategies of growth partnering—branding and rebranding—are both among the most profitable. They compare favorably with the low profit probability yet high cost-effectiveness of the lower right quadrant of the grid. Conversely, they compare less favorably with the higher profit probability, lower cost-effectiveness and aggravated risk of businesses in the upper left quadrant.

Figure 5-3. The profit/cost-efficiency grid.

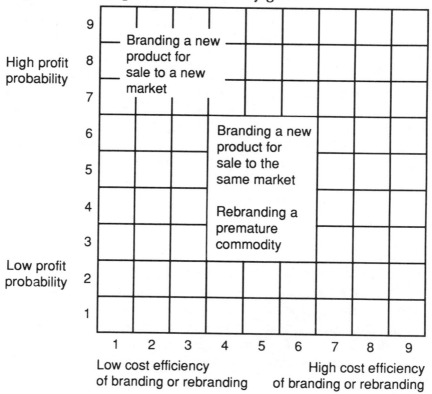

When partners come together to create an entirely new business entity, they will be operating in the upper left quadrant of Figure 5-3. Risk will be high and cost-effectiveness low because so many unfamiliar variables must be planned for. Whenever a business is based on a conjunction of unfamiliarities—a new product or service sold to a new or unfamiliar market—the highest risks and rewards coexist.

Three critical success factors should guide the growth strategies you choose for your partnerships:

1. *The intensity of your investment in terms of the ratio of your total investment in partnered growth to the sales revenue you derive from it.* A low investment base and low intensity typically correspond to high return on investment. You can manipulate two handles to manage return. One handle is profit on sales, which can be managed in two ways: A higher unit price can be charged or a greater volume of goods can be sold at the same price. The second handle on return is to reduce the investment base, which can be accomplished by capital management strategies such as reduced inventory levels; accelerated collections of accounts receivable; reduction of additions to fixed capital; improved utilization of cash resources; and, of course, reduced borrowing made possible by generating capital internally.

To accelerate your profit growth, you must pay close attention to your sales income, watch your costs in relation to sales income, and be miserly about the level of capital you employ to earn your sales income.

The most significant cluster of factors conducive to partnered growth is the relationship between volume, costs, and profit. In the management of this three-way mix, the concept of marginal income plays a pivotal role. Marginal income is sales minus the variable costs of achieving sales. When the marginal income ratio is high, at the 40 percent level or better, fixed costs can usually be easily recovered and growth profits can be accumulated readily from even comparatively small increases in volume anywhere above the break-even point. This is so for two reasons. Fixed costs remain the same regardless of increased volume. And after break-even, profits are earned at a much faster rate than sales since marginal income is translated into profits.

The second most significant group of factors in partnered growth is the twinship of volume and price. The optimal profit-making situation is to sell in volume at a premium price. If you cannot have high volume, you must hold premium price. When volume is small, an inverse relationship prevails between volume and price. The smaller the volume, the more important premium price will be in contributing to profit growth.

2. *Your percentage market share.* Optimal market share is the point at which return on investment is best. Up to this point, return generally increases with market share. This increase will usually be accompanied by a rising rate of investment turnover and a diminishing ratio of marketing expense to sales. Beyond optimal market share, the point of diminishing return on investment will set in.

3. *The quality of your product offering expressed as the sum total of costs invested in a product or system that is being grown at an accelerated rate.* Product quality should not be confused with, nor is it directly proportional to, a product's utility. Overengineered, overcosted products are often the greatest constraints on high return on investment. An overengineered product is one that suffers from excessive quality; that is, it is capable of delivering a greater benefit or more numerous benefits than its market requires or is willing to pay for. You should determine the "enoughness" of the benefits that will satisfy your heavy profit contributors' demand and build to their standards.

Figure 5-4 allows you to enter these three critical success factors into your growth plan.

Targeting Partnerable Opportunities

A customer's operations—the processes by which he makes and markets his products or services—are the entry points for partnering. Which of his profit-centered operations is most suscep-

Figure 5-4. Growth evaluation guidelines.

Business or product ———————— Sold to SIC # ——— Industry classification ———

or consumer life-style ———

1. Investment intensity
   (Total investment/sales)

   Optimal investment/sales ratio = ——%

   Actual investment/sales ratio = ——%   +/– deviation = ——%

2. Market share
   (Percentage penetration/total market)

   Optimal market share = ——%

   Actual market share = ——%   +/– deviation = ——%

3. Product quality
   (Sum total of costs invested)

   Optimal product quality (cost) = $ ——,——,——

   Actual product quality (cost) = $ ——,——,——   +/– deviation = $ ——,——,——

tible to your expertise in making them more productive of revenues and earnings? Which of his cost-centered operations is most susceptible to making them less expensive to manage or maintain? How much more profitable could they be as a result?

The answers to such questions furnish the leads for your partnering. By accessing them in the form of a data base, you can create your asset base of knowledge for growth partnering. As a result, you will be able to see where you can apply your expertise to help your customers grow.

Dresser-Wayne, a supplier of retail management systems for gasoline service stations, databases all of its growth partnerships. It partners on its ability to improve its partners' profits from timely information to station owners on how they can achieve more accurate cost and inventory control and reduce labor.

Dresser-Wayne has equipped itself with a data base in which each of its market segments—major oil companies, independents, and convenience stores—has its own data even though the general benefits that Dresser-Wayne can offer to all three segments are similar: improved profits through increased sales at reduced costs. Specific benefits vary with the market segment. Dresser-Wayne's data is organized around issues such as:

- What is the problem this chain is having at the station level? Is it principally an inventory control problem based on poor cash management? Is it a credit control problem? Are receipts and distribution to blame or is it a question of labor skills, quality or maintenance, or the inefficiency of present station design and resulting customer throughput?

- What are the total costs that a partnership can reduce? What are the total new sales revenues that a partnership can gain? What are the investment offsets required to achieve these results? What net profit will result to the partners? What are the most likely returns on their investments?

An outline of Dresser-Wayne's information base for its partnerships with convenience stores is shown in Figures 5-5 and 5-6.

The problem/opportunity summary in Figure 5-6 shows the monthly profit currently contributed by key outlets in the ABC Convenience Stores chain located in New York State. Positive contributions may indicate partnership opportunities for Dresser-Wayne if they are lower than average; negative contributions may indicate opportunities to reduce or eliminate them.

If a chain's inventory control shows a negative profit contribution or only a small positive contribution to the chain's profit, it can be analyzed as a separate problem in Figure 5-7. A problem of stockout can be intensively evaluated according to its gallonage and dollar values. If Dresser-Wayne believes it can improve them, it can create a partnership proposal that compares the partnership's potential profit improvement with the customer's current situation. Figure 5-5 is used to show the

Figure 5-5. Benefit analysis.

Market segment	Convenience stores	
Customer	ABC Convenience Stores Inc.	
State/Region	New York/Northeast	
Business function	Inventory control	
	Benefits	
	Monthly	*Weekly*
	($000)	*($000)*
Product loss		
Leakage	_____	_____
Vapor	_____	_____
Theft	_____	_____
Out of stock	_____	_____
Excess inventory	_____	_____

Figure 5-6. Problem/opportunity summary.

Market segment	Convenience Stores
Customer	ABC Convenience Stores Inc.
State/Region	New York/Northeast

Monthly profit contribution ($000)

Outlet

    Credit control   _____

    Inventory control   _____

    Cash control   _____

    Staff productivity   _____

    Maintenance   _____

    Throughput efficiency   _____

    Site layout/size   _____

Home office

    Date control and report   _____

    Cash management   _____

    Supervisor productivity   _____

    Communications   _____

    Total contribution/month   _____

    Total contribution/year   _____

dollar benefits that a partnership with Dresser-Wayne can bring to the customer on a weekly and monthly basis for any individual store or for the entire ABC chain. The chain's compulsion to partner will be based on these benefits.

Making the Five Key Assessments

Every partnership plan's data base requires five key assessments: market potential, market penetration, probability of

Figure 5-7. Problem analysis.

Market segment	Convenience stores
Customer	ABC Convenience Stores Inc.
State/Region	New York/Northeast
Business function	Inventory control
Problem	Stockout
Average time out of stock	_____
Number of times out of stock per year	_____
Average number of gallons pumped per hour	_____
Margin per gallon	_____ ¢

product acquisition at various selling prices, cash flow, and the impact of competition on lead time.

1. *Assessing market potential.* Market potential is the upside sales opportunity if every qualified prospect becomes a customer. As such, market potential is a mythical figure. But it is nonetheless valuable as a best-case ceiling in estimating the extent to which market development may be expanded.

2. *Assessing market penetration.* Penetration is the most likely portion of total market potential that is actually being planned for realization at an annual rate. Penetration may be expressed as total sales units or gross sales dollars. In either case, it tells the rate at which share of market is being accumulated.

Penetration is a volume concept. It answers the question "How much?" It is also intimately connected to time. For every market, there is an average number of years required for a product to top out the maximum penetration level on its life-cycle curve. With this number in mind, penetration can be used as an index of maturity since it reveals the extent to which qualified prospects are entering the partnership's market and reaching their heaviest usage rate.

3. *Assessing probability of product acquisition.* Probability is an expression of the likelihood of product acquisition in the near term at various value-to-price relationships. It is based on two factors: needs, which may range from low to high, and benefits perceived for each need, which may be derived from one or more product features.

4. *Assessing cash flow.* A market penetration strategy mix must be responsive to ROI objectives, striving for the maximum cash flow that is consistent with maximizing ROI.

Cash flow is the cash proceeds from earnings minus cash outlays. The projected cash-flow patterns of two alternative market penetration plans illustrate how similar ROIs can generate different streams of cash over a three-year life cycle:

Cash Flow

	Preentry	Year 1	Year 2	Year 3	Three-year cumulative net cash flow
Plan A	(−$20,000)	+$16,000	+$16,000	+$ 4,000	+$16,000
Plan B	(−$20,000)	+$ 4,000	+$ 8,000	+$24,000	+$16,000

Both plans predict the same average three-year ROI of $5,334 per year, or 53 percent. On an ROI basis, there is little to choose between them. But the flow of cash earnings from Plan A promises to recover marketing outlays earlier than Plan B would, enabling a business to go on a more nearly self-sustaining basis beginning with year one instead of waiting until year three.

5. *Assessing the impact of competition on lead time.* The entry of competition marks the end of lead time. During lead time, penetration may be low but profits can be high because premium pricing based on exclusivity can prevail. With the onset of competition, pricing at premium levels may have to give way to commodity pricing and correspondingly lower unit profits. Because of competition's effect on price, it is important to estimate not only a conservative terminal date for lead time but

also the most probable replacement rate at which market penetration will be eroded. This will permit profit projections to be based on relative annual market shares under competitive conditions.

Probability theory may be applied to estimate the end of lead time. Three assumptions may be made: a zero probability that competitive entry will not occur for three years, a 50 percent probability that competition will enter the market within two years, and a zero probability for a competitive end to lead time within year one of commercialization.

Planning Noncommittally for Futures

Partnering is a commitment that tomorrow's growth will be greater than today's. In this sense, partners acknowledge the time value of their business together—that the value of their businesses tomorrow will be greater than today's values only by, or more assuredly by, partnering. The basic decision of partnering is to determine if the growth it promises will be better than going it alone. The second decision is to select the partners who will maximize your growth.

Because it is tomorrow's growth that is on the line in partnering, partnerships deal in futures. Each partner must be able to reach out beyond today's business and ask, "What must our business be like one to three years from now?" This means what markets must we be in a preeminent position to grow, what capabilities must we provide to grow them, how must our capability mix be allocated between ourselves and our partners—which will determine the partners we must ally with—and what are the major competitive partnerships we must be prepared to cope with?

The answers to these questions will compose each collaborator's "partnered growth plan."

Answers that have the best chance of predicting the future can come from constructing an agenda of debatable propositions for you and your potential partners to reconcile together. Figures 5-8 and 5-9 show model propositions for debate be-

Figure 5-8. Debatable propositions for retailers.

1. Instead of customers coming to retailers, retailers and suppliers will increasingly come to customers through telemarketing, credit cards, catalogs, club memberships, faxing, and micro-shops-on-wheels.
2. The percentage of profits from services sold by retailers will continually increase over the percentage of profits from products. Currently separate services such as day care and shopping will be combined so that children and goods can be picked up simultaneously.
3. Self-service credit card purchases will robotize food and beverage retailing and provide access to all stores on a 24-hour daily basis.
4. Nonconsumable rental products such as videotapes and household tools will become a growing portion of retail revenues.
5. Frequent shopper services such as party and event planning, travel planning, and other computerized information-type services will be widely available at retail.
6. All stores will either become or allocate space for boutique-type "convenience stores" just as all banks are becoming convenience banks through automated teller convenience centers.

tween the Gold Teams of a retailer and his suppliers to the food and beverage categories of his stores. The joint resolutions of these debates will predict the future complexion of their partnership.

The debatable propositions are all as-if conjectures, intended to be debated as if they were going to come true as previews of the partnership's future. The models shown in the figures take specific points of view. They say that this is what we think tomorrow will be like today but it is debatable; what do you think? For example, if you are a beverage supplier and we believe that beverages will be robotized for sale on a 24-hour daily basis, are you prepared to help us develop the robotized vending machines, the optimal product mix of flavors and sizes, and the pricing and promotion packages to market your prod-

Figure 5-9. Debatable propositions for food and beverage suppliers.

1. Point-of-sale marketing will increase over media advertising because continuous price and promotion deals and warehouse-type hypermarkets are making retailing hazardous to brand loyalty.
2. Products will fall into two categories: health or entertainment. In-between products will lack preferential positioning or fall into no-man's land. Products that can combine both appeals will be winners.
3. Products will increasingly be sold in prepackaged "systems" with related products of the same or compatible suppliers or with related services such as videocassette rental.
4. Promotions will be continuous and all products will be on some type of "sale" every day.
5. Shopping will follow the 80-20 rule: 80 percent of the repetitive purchases bought weekly will be prepackaged and pre-billed for credit card shoppers, locking in their brand preferences.
6. More sizes and varieties of fewer brands will dominate retail planograms. More planograms will be produced by suppliers who act as category managers.

ucts this way in our stores? What do you have to do? What must we do? Does this strategy fit your concept of your market over the next one to three years? By how much do you believe it can grow our business together?

What if we do not do it? What might our opportunity loss be? Who else is likely to do it? If someone else does it first, what might our opportunity loss be until we can catch up? What if we do it first and it fails—what will it cost us? How long will it take us to recover? How will we recover?

Reaching out into the near-term future brings the partners' strategic planners, corporate and product developers, and business line managers together in new configurations, supported by their financial and information staffs. By hashing and rehashing the major propositions with which the future may most likely confront them, they can test their risks and rewards noncommittally yet realistically.

Asking Self-Appraising Questions

The customers of your partnerships will let you know how good an idea your partnering is. If their reaction is negative, by the time you find out about it, it will probably be too late for you to do anything. The best you can do is to conduct your own semi-final appraisal of your growth plans. You and your partner should ask four questions:

1. Is our growth positioning proprietary enough?
2. Is our return potential high enough?
3. Are our driving forces optimally harnessed?
4. Are our assessment checkpoints properly programmed?

Is Our Plan's Growth Positioning Proprietary Enough?

Growth positioning is the basis for your partnership's marketing. You should assess two considerations:

1. Is our growth positioning the best pairing we can make between our partnership's single most meaningful benefit and the single most meaningful need of its heavy profit-contributor market?
2. Is our growth positioning the most differentiated we can make from our most likely competition?

Is Our Plan's Return Potential High Enough?

Return potential is a way of previewing your partnership's ability to return its investment. You should assess three considerations:

1. Is our profit payoff sufficient to qualify our partnership as an accelerated grower of our businesses?
2. Are our costs in line with our payoff?
3. Have we assumed as close as we can come to 100 percent probability the worst-case impacts on profits, costs, and volume?

Are Our Driving Forces Optimally Harnessed?

Driving forces are your partnership's growth strategies. You should assess two considerations:

1. Do our growth strategies represent the minimal mix of brand-building strategies required to achieve our maximum growth objectives?
2. Are our growth objectives the most significant we can make in terms of our strategies?

Are Our Assessment Checkpoints Properly Programmed?

Checkpoints are your partnership's control stations. You should assess two considerations:

1. Is the staging of our checkpoints front-end-loaded toward the early phases of our partnership's time frame so that we can solve small problems while they are still small and anticipate larger problems with sufficient early warning?
2. Have we tentatively identified the earliest checkpoint where we may have to revise our strategy, and do we have adequate foresight of the strategy revisions we will most likely be required to choose from?

If your plan hangs tough in answer to these four self-appraisal questions you will be able to go to market with increased confidence. Growth will not be preordained, but you will have reduced your risk and protected yourself as best you can against catastrophic failure. You will have made growth more graspable.

To make growth graspable is the function of growth planning. To grasp growth is the function of management. The way to run a successful growth partnership is to put them both together.

6

Product Developing
With Growth Partners

The single most important question to ask about a partnership's product development process in any business is, *Where are the customers in it?* The answer should be "everywhere." Your customers should be in the development process from inception, infusing it with their needs for its contribution to their competitive advantage and their requirements for maximum customer satisfaction. Customers should be present at conception to engineer the genetic code of their needs into each product so that at delivery, and at all key points in between, their parentage is explicit.

If your customers are not partnered with your developers from the dream stage of concept definition and testing through prototype development, product design, product planning, pilot manufacturing, and test installation, you will be postponing all your surprises until the very end when it is too late. As far as your product is concerned, you may have put everything you have into it. But your customers may not be able to get everything they need out of it.

"The customer" should be everywhere in development: in conceptual focus groups, in the laboratory, at the bench, and on the manufacturing line so that the product is the customer's and not yours when it is developed. At each stage, your ultimate criterion of acceptability should be positive responses to the challenge, "Where is the customer in this?"

Making Customer Marks on Development

Where should the customers with whom you partner make their mark? Your customer partners should be assessors of feasibility: How will your new product or service or process fit with our competitive strategy to be market share leader or profit leader or low-cost supplier in our industry? How will it fit our own customers' needs for competitiveness? How timely will it be—will it still be on the leading edge by the time we can install it or apply it or sell it? Will it be a one-shot item or will there be follow-on products and services that will form an integrated system? Will it meet open standards or will it be so proprietary that we will be locked in? How serviceable will it be? What quality assurance will we have?

What support will be provided to meet legal and regulatory approvals? When will our people be trained and by whom and how? What dates can we count on for design verification, reliability assurance, manufacturability validation, and final cost estimates?

When you bring a customer in as your development partner, you must be prepared to change the development process from start to finish. At the start, your concept of feasibility will have to be broadened to include customer competitiveness as well as operational performance. "Will it work?" is no longer sufficient. You will have to add such questions as:

- ▲ Will it work *to reduce customer costs?* Which ones? How much? How soon?
- ▲ Will it work *to expand customer revenues?* From which lines of business? Sold to which markets? How much? How soon?

Your concept of performance specifications will also have to be broadened:

- ▲ How much reliability will be required to maintain or regenerate customer competitiveness? What are the best

ways to ensure it? Build in redundancy, use modularity for easy disassembly and parts replacement, build in capabilities for self-diagnosis and repair, create an enhanced training program, or provide stand-by units?
▲ How much product-family commonality is necessary?

As you build the customer in, you install customer specifications for just the correct degree of "enoughness" in your product quality—not too little to serve customer needs for competitiveness nor too much to defeat customer competitiveness and your own by providing excess quality whose costs cannot be reclaimed by either of you.

Serving Six Partnered Purposes

When you bring your customers into development, their partnering should serve six purposes for both of you:

1. *Shift development resources at the 80 percent point.* Your customer partners can help you determine when to migrate your scarce talent and financial resources from being further invested in current technology curves into new and discontinuous ones. The point where approximately 80 percent of your customers' commercial value has been achieved is called the shift point in Figure 6-1. When you reach it, customers can give you the assurance you need to start stage one of a new development cycle instead of sponsoring stage two of the original development in an attempt to squeeze out its elusive remaining 20 percent of value. In this way, your partnerships can always be developing new leading-edge curves instead of becoming stuck reiterating favorite technologies or massaging comfortably familiar applications.

2. *Recognize enoughness in value creation.* Customers represent practical limits on pushing product development curves, helping you know when to get off each of them at the point where the value for the customer has become "good enough."

Figure 6-1. Plotting the optimal shift point.

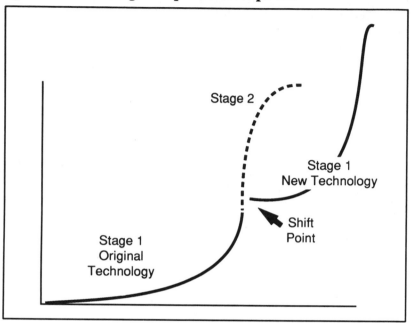

As Figure 6-2 shows, this will help you avoid the temptation to keep sponsoring a product all the way up to its theoretical limits just because your technical people think they can do so or are afraid that someone else will do so if they do not. By enforcing a "service ceiling" on development, your customers can safeguard you against the lure of chasing after the excesses of six sigma quality at the 99.9997 level of perfection when they would be either nonproductive of commensurate customer competitiveness or so cost-ineffective that their benefits would be self-canceling.

3. *Cash in on fads.* Customers can open two kinds of opportunity windows for you, one short-term and the other longer. Short-term opportunties are fads, coming and going without a great deal of predictability. If you consistently miss out on them or get in on them so late that they can no longer be fully capitalized, you risk truncating your short-term growth curves as

Figure 6-2. Recognizing "good enoughness."

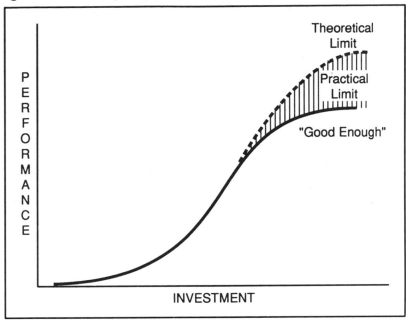

Figure 6-3 shows. Each growth spike that is truncated represents opportunity costs whose lost value to you can add up to as much as one-third of your annual revenues regularly realized from new product commercialization.

4. *Avoid development lag.* If you miss a curve, represented by the "missing link" in the chain of successive commercializable developments shown in Figure 6-4, you invite three problems. You risk the temporary loss of market position while you are without an entry. You fall into a gap in your ability to command premium price margins as your old entries become mature commodities and you have no "hot boxes" to take their place. And once you drop the ball, you may never regain your development momentum or your market repute. With customers as an incremental idea source, you can reduce the chance of development lags whose effects on staff retention and motivation, market position, and maximizing margins can be disastrous.

Figure 6-3. Cashing in on fads.

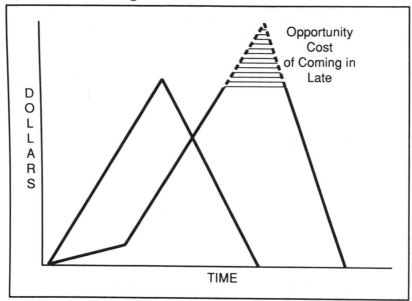

5. *Calculate initial cost–ongoing cost tradeoffs.* Customers can help you make more optimal tradeoffs between acceptable initial acquisition costs of new products and their continuing life-cycle costs of ownership that include operating, maintenance, service, repair, and replacement expenses. There are three questions that customers can help you answer in trying to achieve the ideal relationship shown in Figure 6-5:

- ▲ How high can acquisition cost be and still be justified by low ownership costs?
- ▲ How soon must the premium on high acquisition costs be repayable by ownership cost savings?
- ▲ How many years constitute an acceptable "useful life cycle" over which acquisition costs can be traded off?

6. *Prevent nonproducts.* When customers are not partnered in the new product development process, the result is often a

Figure 6-4. Losing out from development lag.

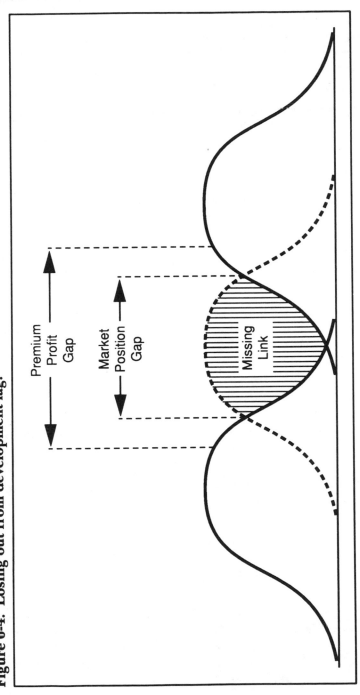

Figure 6-5. Achieving the ideal cost tradeoff.

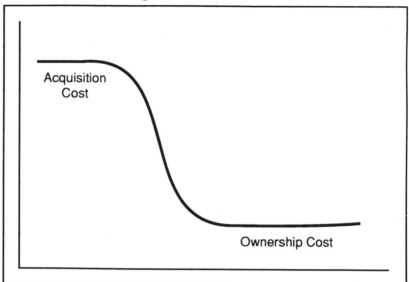

nonproduct. A nonproduct is a form of scrap: highly machined, precision-made scrap, perhaps, frequently representing an ingenious rearrangement of molecules or microchips and generally unlike anything on the market, but scrap nonetheless.

Nonproducts are the natural result of a customer-deprived technology where things are made because they can be made or because somebody says they cannot; because competitors are making them or they are not; or because no one else has the technology or controls the market or the distribution or the patents. All of these drive forces put the development process into a prescrap mode.

DuPont's venture into Corfam, a poromeric plastic material, shows what can happen when the development process lacks customer input. Corfam cost $100 million in 1963 dollars, never yielded a profit, and was discontinued in seven years. The material, which was produced as the result of more than 200 human-years of research and testing, appeared to DuPont to offer significant benefits as a leather substitute.

Corfam was a victim of four incorrect market and product assumptions. DuPont's basic assumption, from which the other three assumptions were derived, was that the shoe industry would be Corfam's major opportunity based on projections of a substantial leather shortage by 1982. While less leather would be available on a per-consumer basis, huge increases in footwear consumption were contemplated. This would create a "leather gap" for about 30 percent of all the shoes required in the 1980s.

Once the so-called leather gap was assumed, it was decided that the greatest opportunity to plug it with a high-priced leather substitute would be in shoes selling in the $20 to $40 price range. In preparing to penetrate this market, DuPont made three additional assumptions without help from its customers or retailers.

First, DuPont assumed that Corfam would offer a cost advantage to shoe manufacturers. At a price of $1.05 per square foot, Corfam projections showed an acceptable share of market could be conquered from leather even though initial use would be restricted to shoes priced from $20 up. But this price proved to be inhibitive. Shoe manufacturers could have told DuPont that Corfam offered no significant cost advantage over leather and no compensating production cost advantage, but they were never asked. DuPont further assumed that mass production would lower Corfam's price. But in scaling up from pilot operations, Corfam never was produced at the predicted cost.

Second, DuPont assumed that six very important user benefits would outweigh one "moderately" important deficit. Corfam shoes offered breathability, water-repellency, scuff resistance, and a permanent shine. DuPont also believed that durability was a major benefit, even though apparel markets were moving away from durability toward disposability, and that shape retention also was desirable. Unfortuntely, shape retention, which was the result of Corfam's plastic "memory," so effectively prevented the material from permanently stretching to accommodate the wearer's foot that Corfam shoes had to be broken in all over again after each wearing.

Third, DuPont assumed that Corfam's competition would come from domestic leather shoes. Shoe retailers and customers could have told DuPont that competition would be more likely to come from imports from Spain and Italy that offered Continental styling at low prices and from other synthetics, especially low-end nonbreathable polyvinyls, but they were never asked.

It is highly unusual that, at one and the same time, mass competition would have come from low-priced imports, that low-end nonbreathable vinyl would have been accepted by a market that had always insisted on breathability, that the discomfort in use caused by a material's memory would have canceled out several genuine benefits, and that technical problems in a high-technology company could have prevented predicted-cost projections from being realized over a seven-year time frame. Statisticians like to assume that compensating factors will occur to prevent multiple problems or errors from falling on the same side. The major contribution of the Corfam experience is to cast doubt on this assumption.

Codeveloping Your Customer Teams

Taking on customer partners as codevelopers acknowledges their unique contribution: only they can know "what the customer wants"—what costs he must control and what costs he can accept in return for controlling them; what revenues he must realize, what margins he must earn on them, and what costs he can accept to bring them in. Only the customer knows the priorities of his rank order of critical success issues that he must deal with and the role that innovative products and services can play—and can be affordably funded to play—in improving the contributions they must make to his competitiveness. This knowledge is irreplaceable. It is available nowhere else and if you deny it for your partnerships you will be making a gift of it to your competitors.

Since there is no single customer who represents all customers, you must be prepared to partner with representatives from each of your major customers. And since no single representative can speak for all the business functions and lines of business that can be affected by your development process, you must be prepared to partner with representatives from several functions and lines of business.

As full-fledged members of your development teams, customers can play roles in which they propose and dispose in real time while your development process is on stream and suscep-tible to invigoration. They will be building for themselves just as you are building for them. They bring to the party the over-riding guidelines of customer acceptance, something that you and your partners can assume only at your peril.

7

Business Venturing
With Growth Partners

Ventures represent a quantum leap beyond new product development, seeking to create entirely new businesses based on new technologies and new applications of technologies that can create a new market. While product development and engineering are concerned with maximizing the yield of an existing technology, venturing concerns itself with commercializing emergent technologies for markets that may be nonexistent at the outset of a partnership or are at least not being competitively served.

Bringing potential customers in as venture partners can reduce the average risk that six to nine of every ten ventures will fail. Most of them fail not because their technology does not work but because there turns out to be no growth market for their products or services: in other words, they enhance no important competitive advantage for their customers or their enhancement is not important enough to justify their price plus the attendant costs of ownership.

If you can partner your venture processes with their most likely customers, front-ending their contributions and "getting to yes or no" fast, you can help ensure that the one Big Winner you need from each set of ten candidates is quickly identified and more quickly and surely brought to profitable commercialization.

The main objective of customer partnering in the venture

process ought to be to increase the likelihood of Big Winners, not simply to avoid losers. Customers can help with both. But their competitiveness as well as yours is best served by stepping up the number of winners and speeding up the cycle by which they are generated.

Using customer partners to help *screen in* Big Winners rather than only *screen out* probable future failures puts a positive cast on venturing. It will be your way of institutionalizing the belief that the major risks in venturing are not those posed by total losses, break-even businesses, or even marginally profitable businesses. The worst risk is the opportunity cost of the Big Winner that gets away because it is not ventured.

Planning a Venture Process

The process for partnering the growth of Big Winner venture businesses must have two objectives. One is a minimum hit ratio of one Big Winner from every eight candidates. The other is a minimum survival-to-loss ratio of three profit-making survivors for every two whose profits are lost to break-even or failure. Achieving these two ratios will assure you that the venture process is working.

The One-in-Eight Hit Ratio

In order to be cost-effective, the lowest acceptable yield of a venture process must be one Big Winner from every eight candidates. This will enable growth to be predictable, consistent, and self-financing through the recycling of profits. It will also allow growth to become familiar, making it the rule rather than an exception. If the mean time between Big Winners is stretched thinner than one in eight, growth becomes chancy and sporadic; it loses its rhythm as a planned, periodic event and the partners may never be able to pay back their development costs.

Out of every cycle's eight growth candidates, a maximum of three can be lost between the time the selection process starts and the final cut begins. Of the five survivors, the most likely result, shown in Figure 7-1, is:

- ▲ One Big Winner, a new business with a minimum 10 to 30 percent annual rate of growth over its first three years and a minimum annual gross revenue of $15 to $35 million by year three
- ▲ Two Profitmakers, new businesses with lower annual rates of growth than the Big Winners and a lesser annual gross revenue contribution
- ▲ One Break-even business, a no-return business that pays back its investment
- ▲ One Failure, a nonbusiness that does not achieve break-even by year three

Figure 7-1. One-in-eight hit ratio.

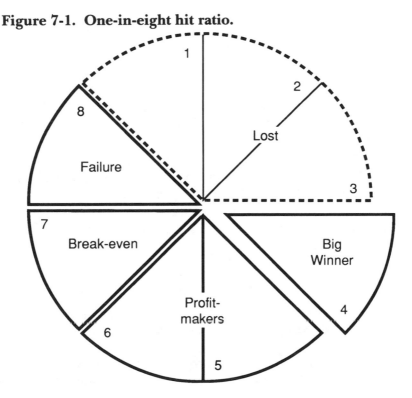

These outcomes can be regarded as a normal statement of the sources and distribution of growth funds. The Big Winner and the two Profitmakers are the capital sources for each venture cycle. They fund the partners' expended earnings. In addition, they pay for each cycle's investment by allowing it to be internally financed. The two remaining businesses, the Breakeven and the Failure, are costs. The Break-even business is an opportunity cost. The Failure is also a direct cost.

The Three-to-Two Survival-to-Loss Ratio

At each phase of a venture cycle, rationalization takes place. When a cycle begins, all the candidates look good. On a judgmental basis, it is often hard to choose between them; all eight may have the aura of Big Winners, encouraging among the partners a euphoric "bonanza psychology" that will be disabused at the cycle's first turn.

After the cycle's screening phase, the partners should expect that only six of the original eight growth candidates will still survive. After testing, five of the six candidates should still be survivors. After commercialization, three of the five survivors should be moneymakers. From among them, Figure 7-2 shows the emergence of the Big Winner.

This survival-to-loss ratio dictates the need for starting each venture cycle with eight prime candidates. No lesser number will yield the requisite three moneymakers. Nothing other than truly prime candidates will survive the winnowing process to yield one Big Winner. Unless there is a continuing supply of premier business opportunities to put into the hopper, the partners will be unable to count on producing a Big Winner from each cycle. As either the quantity of candidates diminishes or their quality decreases, the odds against winners rise automatically.

Selecting a Selection Procedure

You and your partners will need a joint venture selection process. Many procedures exist, ranging from a simplistic injunction

Figure 7-2. Three-to-two survival-to-loss ratio.

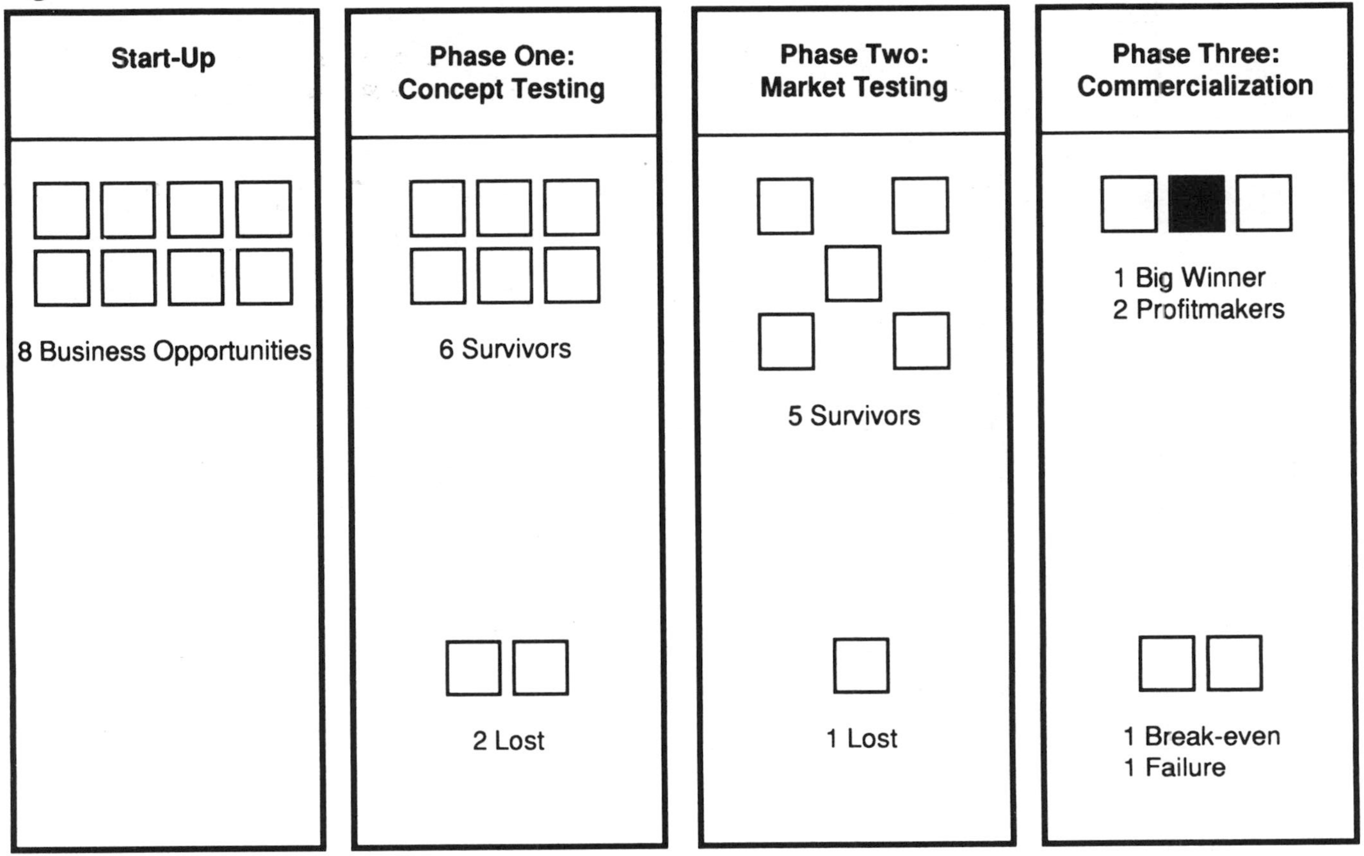

Start-Up	Phase One: Concept Testing	Phase Two: Market Testing	Phase Three: Commercialization
8 Business Opportunities	6 Survivors 2 Lost	5 Survivors 1 Lost	1 Big Winner 2 Profitmakers 1 Break-even 1 Failure

such as "All venture products must fit existing distribution channels" to mechanistic methods such as "formidable formulas" and "partners' sandwiches."

Formidable Formulas

A *formidable formula* is a method for representing the probable marketability of a venture product or service by assigning arbitrary values to market, engineering, and research estimates.

The chances of a venture's technical and commercial success are expressed as percentages, with 100 percent equaling 1. Average annual sales volume is expressed in units. Price is the net sales price per unit in dollars. Cost is the total dollar cost per unit. Commercial life is the square root of the estimated number of years over which average annual sales volume can be expected to remain approximately the same. Total costs are the total dollars invested in product development, including research, design, manufacturing, and marketing. The higher the priority category the formula yields, the stronger a product's claim to selection.

An example shows how the formula works. Assume that engineering and research estimate that the chance of actually developing a product is 80 percent. Marketing estimates the chance of commercial success at 60 percent. Average annual sales are estimated at about 20,000 units per year during a nine-year life cycle. Net selling price will be about $120. Total cost including materials, labor, and overhead will be about $87. Research has cost $50,000; design, $140,000; manufacturing, development, tooling, and facilities, $230,000; and marketing development, including advertising and promotion, $50,000. Total investment is $470,000. In this case, the venture earns a 6, which is good, but not great.

$$\frac{0.8 \times 0.6 \times 20,000 \times (120-87) \times 9}{470,000}$$
$$= \text{category } 6$$

Partners' Sandwich

A *partners' sandwich* is a method of representing the probable marketability of a venture product or service by surrounding it with a top slice of *grandview criteria* and a bottom slice of *keyhole criteria.*

The top slice calls for the partners to take an overall view of two things: what rewards the partners require to achieve their growth objectives and where rewards of this nature can be found. These criteria, which answer the policy questions of "What?" and "Where?", may be called *grandview criteria.* The bottom slice of the selection sandwich calls for the partners to take an intensive, up-close view of potential business opportunities and judge whether they represent businesses "for us." These criteria are based principally on technical and marketing considerations. Because they apply short strokes to product selection, they may be called *keyhole criteria.*

Grandview Criteria: Is There a Business Here?

Every partnership needs a set of grandview criteria to start its product, service, or business selection process. These are the criteria that set gross boundaries for growth in two categories: the dimensions of the rewards required as a return for the partners' investment and the type of businesses that will most likely yield these rewards. A list of grandview criteria for a consumer packaged-goods business is shown in Figure 7-3. Figure 7-4 shows a grandview list for a partnered venture into industrial manufacturing.

Each partnership will have to work out its own grandview criteria for growth. Criteria must authentically reflect the partnership's personality, its industry background, and the degree of venturesomeness that characterizes the partners' management style. One management's grandview may be another management's pettyview.

Keyhole Criteria: Is There a Business Here for Us?

When a candidate business meets a partnership's grandview criteria, the partners must get down to the nitty-gritty. This requires a much more finite set of standards to obtain a keyhole view of a new business opportunity.

Figure 7-3. Grandview criteria for a consumer packaged-goods business.

---

1. Reward characteristics

1.1. A business must offer a minimum average annual growth rate of 8 percent over five years.

1.2. A business must have the potential of developing a minimum $25 million in net sales or $5 million in profit before taxes, or both, by the fifth year of market life.

1.3. A business must have the potential of yielding a minimum 30 percent pretax return on investment.

2. Industry characteristics

2.1. A business must have a high potential acceptance for new branded products and services that have high consumer repeat rates and high retail turnover rates.

2.2. A business must position mass, middle-majority homemakers as its major customers and preferably also involve the homemakers' families.

2.3. A business must lend itself to standardization of products and services, yet possess opportunity for a meaningful product or marketing difference that can be mass advertised and mass merchandised.

Among the three categories of keyhole criteria, one category encompasses marketing, including a set of standards for evaluating market acceptability of a venture's product and service characteristics, sales and distribution characteristics, and competitive characteristics that the partners judge to be required for Big Winner success. A model list of keyhole marketing criteria is shown in Figure 7-5.

A second category of keyhole criteria are the technical standards that a product or business must meet, along the lines of the model shown in Figure 7-6.

A third category of criteria for keyhole selection is com-

Figure 7-4. Grandview criteria for an industrial manufacturing venture.

1. **Reward characteristics**

   1.1. A minimum of five times capital appreciation over investment must be realized during the first two to three years of commercial life, growing to a minimum of ten times investment over a five-to-seven-year life cycle.

   1.2. A minimum 35 to 40 percent gross margin on sales must be achievable.

2. **Industry characteristics**

   2.1. The industry must offer a demand base that grows faster than the real average annual growth of the GNP during periods of expansion and declines more slowly than the GNP during recessions.

   2.2. The industry must display two or more inflation-resistant characteristics such as strong demand growth, low labor costs as a percentage of revenues, small capital requirements, minimal investment in fixed assets, high profit margins, and the ability to protect them by raising prices as costs escalate.

   2.3. The industry must not be dependent on scarcity-prone raw materials or consume unusually large energy resources.

   2.4. A strong current market need must exist, and it must be susceptible to rapid development that can contribute substantial short-term profit growth.

   2.5. A specific preemptive market position must be achievable within three years, commanding a minimum 20 percent share of market.

posed of financial objectives. When venture objectives are used as criteria, they should be translated into the style of the following two examples:

   1. To be venturable, a business must promise a minimum average pretax return on investment of 30 percent over

(Text continued on page 114.)

Figure 7-5. Keyhole marketing criteria.

1. **Partnership compatibility characteristics**

   1.1. Product and service systems must be compatible with market perceptions of the partnership's image in regard to ethical standards, social responsibility, and environmental protection.

   1.2. Product and service systems must be compatible with the partnership's marketing knowledge and within the scope of marketing management's capabilities.

   1.3. Product and service systems must be free from socially restrictive or legally regulated limitations on marketing.

2. **Market characteristics**

   2.1. The market must be in the growth phase of its life cycle so that a minimum 5 percent increase in gross sales volume can be forecast over a five-year time frame.

   2.2. The market must conform to the demand characteristics of a segment composed of a minimum of 5 million households that generate a minimum $50 million retail market.

   2.3. The value of each 1 percent market share must be a minimum of $2,500,000.

   2.4. The market must provide a noncyclical or countercyclical stream of earnings.

   2.5. The market must not require more than a maximum $10 million direct marketing investment during Year One, or an investment that will not exceed a 1:5 ratio of spending share to market share.

   2.6. Market acceptance must be strong enough to provide a minimum 10 percent share of the market by Year Three and a minimum 20 percent share by Year Five.

3. **Product and service system characteristics**

   3.1. Products and services must possess a brandable competitive difference that is patentable, that preempts satisfaction of an important market need, and that is advertisable in a way that allows user benefits to be perceived as superior to direct competition and therefore deserving a premium price.

3.2. Products and services must possess line and category extension capability into coordinated families of product and service systems. No business should be a one-product business.

3.3. Products and services must be sufficiently future-oriented to promise a minimum five-year life cycle that will sustain a high rate of profitable sales against competition throughout its duration.

3.4. Products and services must not incur more than a maximum $2 million total development cost up to the point of national launch.

4. **Sales and distribution characteristics**

4.1. Products and services must be compatible with salesforce capability.

4.2. Products and services must be compatible with existing channels of distribution.

4.3. Products and services must be compatible with currently used advertising media.

4.4. Product and service systems must not require more than a maximum three-year period to achieve full national distribution from the time of roll-out.

5. **Competitive characteristics**

5.1. To ensure sufficient lead time of freedom from competitive replication, product and service systems must promise a minimum one-year period of proprietary marketing grace derived from technical or marketing preemption, patents, or regulatory agency sanction.

5.2. If an established market is to be penetrated, it must not be "owned" by a single supplier. The market share of the top two competitors should not exceed 40 percent. If there are more than two leaders, their combined market share should not exceed 60 percent. The market should not be so atomized that there is no leader with less than a 15 percent share.

5.3. The market should not be subject to private-brand competition that holds more than a 20 percent share.

Figure 7-6. Keyhole technical criteria.

1. The business must be dependent on proved corporate technical expertise and be completely free of dependence on technological breakthrough discoveries.
2. To prove affordable technical feasibility, a working prototype must be producible for a maximum $100,000 investment within one year.
3. Patent protection must be achievable.
4. A maximum approval time of eighteen months by federal regulatory agencies must be achievable.
5. For early and consistent standardization to be achieved, maximum quality control must be assured for ingredients, process, and product engineering.
6. Adaptation of output to automated mass production must be assured.

---

   its first three years, with a minimum average aftertax return of 20 percent.
2. A venture business must promise a minimum $10 million gross retail sales volume by year three, with a minimum $5 million net sales yield and a minimum $1 million profit before taxes.

Selection criteria tend to proliferate in direct ratio to the insecurity of the partners. Failure is avoided by avoiding venturing because nothing can be found that meets the criteria. To avoid criteria block, it is helpful to construct a "quick screen" composed only of minimal criteria.

A quick screen economizes the venture evaluation process. A candidate that meets the screen's minimal criteria can be looked at intensively as soon as it passes through. Similarly, candidates that fail to meet minimal criteria can be discarded without unwarranted appraisal or an excessive number of over-the-shoulder wistful glances.

A model quick screen of partnerable ventures is shown in Figure 7-7. It contains six criteria, which is the upper limit of

Figure 7-7. Quick screen criteria.

---

1. Minimum 30 percent pretax return on investment.
2. Minimum 20 percent aftertax return by Year Three.
3. Minimum $10 million gross retail sales potential, to yield $5 million net sales and a minimum $2 million profit before taxes by Year Two, with growth potential to a minimum $25 million net sales and $5 million profit before taxes by Year Five.
4. Products marketable to a minimum of 5 million households through supermarket retail distribution and television advertising distribution.
5. Products brandable at a premium price/value relationship.
6. Business nature and style compatible with partnership concept of ethical management and proper social concern.

---

what can be considered minimal. Three of the criteria are concerned with financial considerations. A fourth criterion ensures a venture's market orientation, a fifth forces an early judgment on the ability of a venture's product and service systems to become branded at a premium price, and the sixth relates a venture to the partners' concepts of themselves as good corporate citizens.

Phasing a Venture

Each venture process is a four phase cycle. It starts with data on a potential business opportunity, proceeds to testing a series of potential solutions to realize the opportunity in the most cost-effective manner, creates a single "best solution" from intensive due diligence on its fit, functionality, and financial impacts on customer profitability, and then makes a case for the solution to become a business. Figure 7-8 shows the phase-by-phase progression of this cycle.

The data base of potential business opportunities for venturing should act as a repository for high-gain commercial con-

Figure 7-8. Venture phasing process.

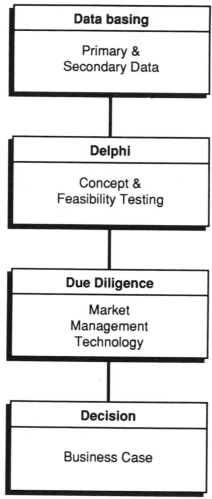

cepts. A concept is a statement of proposed value from a non-existent product or service that is expressed as if it is already deliverable—in other words, as a prepositioning statement. A simplified concept statement for a potential "best solution" is shown in Figure 7-9.

The partners need to create and circulate multiple concept

Figure 7-9. Model concept statement.

Batch production of customized products as small as single units can now be cost-effectively manufactured, even in between mass production runs. Switchover and switchback can be automatically accomplished within 100 nanoseconds, reducing practical downtime to zero. Productivity is improved an average of 5 to 7 percent while costs can be reduced up to $10,000 per shift. These results are accomplished by a flexible manufacturing system (FMS) that employs computerized robots guided by expert system software. The FMS workstations require maintenance on the average of once every 100,000 hours and need no human attendants to operate, service, or change programs. An FMS of this type can be installed on-line for approximately $100,000 and can return the investment in full within six months.

statements internally within the venture and also externally through a serial process of reiteration. This is a form of the Delphi method, which seeks an ever-narrowing, step-by-step evaluation for each concept: what are its perceived assets and liabilities, how do they compare with competitive concepts, what is their likelihood of commercialization as a Big Winner, who are its most likely users, and what is its most probable value-to-price relationship based on its most probable contribution to user value?

Concept statements, together with concept advertising and projections of costs and benefits, help point the way to solutions that are worthy of more intensive due diligence. This will allow the partners to prepare a business case that will serve as a platform for a venture's business plan.

Operating as a Venture Team

Venturing for customer growth requires partnered teams composed of technical, manufacturing, marketing, and financial members. This type of mix ensures that venture opportunities will be created and assessed in a multidisciplinary manner, assaying each potential opportunity from the points of view of scientific feasibility, manufacturability, and profitable marketability. The contributions of customer members helps guarantee that each venture will have takers at its conclusion. Venture partnerships should be organized as if they were a business, operating according to a business plan, a budgeted timetable, and a clearly articulated vision for their eventual market position. By working in a businesslike environment, the venturers will be simulating the real world of operating and financial responsibilities into which their products and services will have to fit. Yet these attributes will have to be combined with a third characteristic of organizational autonomy if the full technical and entrepreneurial business talents of the venture teams are to be realized.

The best organization structure for venturing is the "skunk works" model of task team that is separately staffed and housed, independently budgeted, and loosely controlled by exception from its partners' normal oversight constraints. Periodic progress reports should be sufficient to prove that the venturers are on plan and on budget. Intervention should only be by exception to planned progress.

The "we-ness" of the venture partners is crucial to their success. They must be able to identify their venture as their own, become fiercely loyal to it, and immune from all other performance evaluations except the successful achievement of their business plan. By operating an exclusive organization connected only by a dotted-line relationship to their cosponsors and working under their own self-imposed standards of performance, their individual and team best efforts can be liberated.

The skunk works concept suggests not only their exclusiveness but the undesirability of having anyone violate it who is "here from headquarters to help you." Minimal interference, minimal reporting, and maximum freedom are the optimal formula for venture skunking.

In order to justify its unique free-form status, venture co-managers should be business managers, not technicians. Their drive must be profit based and they will be under the gun to see to it that every technical specification is responsive to a customer need for improved competitiveness as well as supplier profitability.

The heart of a skunk works is the venture's business plan, not the technology that will emerge or the application that it will empower when the plan is fulfilled. The plan must make clear the difference between outcomes that are workable and operable on the one hand and those that are commercializable because they are profitable on the other. To achieve the first without the second is to bring home a failed venture.

8

Problem-Solving in Growth Partnerships

Each partnership will bring its own problems to the table. Three problems occur so predictably that you should have a going-in position on them before you sit down:

1. Dealing with the question of mutual trust, which is so fundamental that it has become colloquialized as the "T-question"
2. Managing people changes in your partnerships and compensating for the eventual loss of your "founding partners"
3. Controlling the downsides of partnering

Dealing With the Trust Question

Mutual competitive advantage is the drive force of growth partnering. Trust is its soul. Partners typically deal with the T-question by suspending their mistrust rather than creating a strategy for mutual trust. But trust that is initially deferred can later become mistrust conferred.

A trust strategy protects the partners against themselves. It helps them safeguard the fiduciary responsibility they take on when they come together to grow new business.

The ultimate risk of betraying a partner's trust is the loss of a grower, one of the small number of major suppliers or customers that has the power to make you significantly more competitive. Finding yourself involuntarily departnered from a growth source is an unaffordable price to pay for anything, let alone the negative values of perfidy or delinquency. In the short run, a partner is irreplaceable. If you become known as untrustworthy, partners will remain unattainable in the long run as well. The question "Who will be left to grow you?" will become unanswerable.

Some "friction costs" are inevitable between partners. As much as possible, they should be discounted in advance. Despite the mutual issues and concerns that bring partners together, suppliers and customers will always retain many separate and sometimes conflicting interests on which they must act without reference to their partnerships. Each partner should expect the other to take advantage of opportunities that are outside the bounds of the partnership but may affect it tangentially, as well as understand that actions appearing to be deviations from either the intent or the operations of an alliance need not render it invalid.

The higher up you go in the hierarchies of partner managers, the greater unthinkability of betraying trust you are likely to find. It is so clearly a lose-lose proposition that trust becomes instinctive, not requiring consideration. Concern about trust exists principally at the middle levels of business function managers, business line managers, and their support staffs. This is where closely held secrets abound and where all information is likely to be regarded as confidential and therefore "owned." In many companies, especially technology-based businesses, it is not a question of what is regarded as confidential but what is not. Sometimes even categorizing what is confidential is confidential.

Even though it is generally easy to gain intellectual agreement that betrayal of trust is pointless, "our data" does not automatically become "your data," "our plans" "your plans," or "our people" "your business growers." No one goes from being an outsider to being accepted overnight as an insider to whom every man would entrust his "wallet and wife." What Xerox calls an "Open Kimono" policy toward its partners is accomplished by earning one peek at a time so that both the peekers and peekees can get accustomed to coping with their new responsibility.

There are two major areas of mutual concern in every partnership. What if they get to know our proprietary data; what will they do with it—will they reveal it to one of our competitors? And what if they get a look at our long-range plans; will they fall into the wrong hands and come back to haunt us when someone uses them against us?

The best trust strategy is to convert only what the partners need that is "mine" and "yours" at the outset into *ours* and to make everything that their partnership creates *ours* from its inception. Once a partnership acquires an asset base of its own, the partners have something to protect, preserve, and defend that represents their mutual property. The partnership's joint data base belongs to them. The partnership's joint plan, with its mutual growth objectives and cooperative strategies, is their plan. Well over half the data base for every partnership must typically be newly generated by the partners simply because neither of them will have had a reason to know its contents beforehand. The partnership's plan will always be brand new. The newness and mutual work that goes into these two major areas of trust will help to make them "ours" at once.

Trust can be made more acceptable if it is invested in a trust strategy, not in people. The strategy should limit access to need, base need on position descriptions, and put self-interest at risk as the penalty for unauthorized internal distribution or external disclosure. The question "Who will grow you?" should be the mandate for trustworthiness.

The partner's mindset comes more naturally to managers who are consultative to begin with and therefore find it easy to regard customers and suppliers as their clients. They progress rapidly from being me-oriented to a we-and-us frame of reference. Other managers are more competitive than cooperative. They regard themselves parochially as their own clients. For them, partnering their mindsets so they can trust someone else will be accelerated by learning to ask questions like these before they make major decisions:

> If I were my partner, would I share this information? If so, why? If not, why not?
>
> What will the most likely impact of sharing and not sharing, both positive and negative, be on my partner?
>
> How can I share with my partner and still protect myself?
>
> If my partner did not share this kind of information wih me, how would I react?

Managing People Changes

It is a moot point whether customer people change job assignments and move around, or out of, their corporations more often than their supplier people who partner with them. But there is no doubt that people come and go at frequent enough intervals on both sides to make long-term partnering impossible in many relationships and difficult in others. Whereas there is no way that you can control how your partners' customers manage their human resources, you can control your own resources in ways that can maximize the value of partner continuity.

In order to take advantage of the fact that repetition is the mother of knowledge, your people who partner should have longevity in their assignments if the concept of partnering is to have validity. Companies do not partner—only people do. Partnering takes time. Your salespeople and support staffs who rotate through customer assignments or market segments, business-unit managers who rotate through departments or divisions, and headquarters people who move in and out exacerbate the shufflings that are always going on in their partners' businesses. Founding partners can quickly give way to second and third generation relationships that retain little if any of the partnering commitments that got things started in the first place.

Eventually, nobody may be left who embodies, let alone remembers, the original reason to ally for mutual growth.

If you hope to grow from partnering, you should make it a point of policy to enforce the continuity of each of your major customer partnerships. If there is going to be one member of your joint partner teams who has persistence, you should want him or her to be one of your own people, not your customer's. This will give you three advantages in managing your partnering for growth:

1. The de facto "managing partner" will be your own man or woman, who will become the senior officer of the partnership based on experience.
2. Your senior partner will contain the conscience of the partnership, preserving its commitment and symbolizing its dedication and perpetuation.
3. The partnership's historical "memory" will be yours, safeguarding its business track record in one mind that can give it true perspective and make its hard-won experience projectable into the future.

Knowing a partner's business is implicitly a function of continuity. So is the ability to see trends in his industry, to project them ahead with some reasonable degree of confidence, and to anticipate their outcomes at a level that is a good deal better than chance. Without experience, none of these things are possible. No matter how rich your partnerships' data bases may be, nothing can replace the fingertip feel for a business that comes from having had the same pair of hands around it for a considerable amount of time.

Inevitably, of course, change will have to occur in your own partnership staffing. When it does, it should be preplanned. The "next partner" should be moved into place gradually, learning his or her way under the partner-in-place's tutelage and getting accustomed to his customer partners-to-be. As the transition telescopes, the new partner will assume more of the privileges and responsibilities of the role and your mentor can retain a consultative capacity that makes sure everything goes smoothly. No transition can be perfectly seamless. On both sides, everyone will have favorite partners. As you grow your customer partners, you can follow your favorites up or across their corporate ladders—or they will take you with them—and create your partnerships on new levels.

Defending Against Departnering

The lesson of the Linda Effect described in Chapter 1 is that partners must usually departner themselves. Third-party pretenders are rarely able to departner them. The bonded cohesion of original partners is always greater than the potential adhesion of a new customer or a new supplier. As a result, partnerships in place are more often lost than won. The most common reason is that the supplier partner stops partnering.

Growth partnerships depend on achieving mutual profit-improvement objectives that are based on customer growth. If a supplier partner forgets this golden rule and puts his own growth ahead of his customer, or appears to, the relationship will take on two objectives instead of one. This will make it untenable.

If a supplier partner appears to want to profit more or sooner than his customer, or if he actually desires these objectives, he will be departnering himself. He will also be departnering if he appears willing to sacrifice customer competitiveness for the sake of his own, such as by pushing his own products or services when they would be more likely to diminish rather than expand customer profits. Malfeasance is one danger. Misfeasance is the other, occurring when the supplier fails to envision future growth opportunities that competitive partnerships are able to see more clearly and preempt for themselves, or if he encourages investments in the wrong future.

Supplier partners must grow their customers first, foremost, and forever. This is done by maintaining a continuing presentation and implementation of profit-improvement projects with customer managers, sharing an evergreen flow of information with them about how their competitiveness can be advanced, and establishing a reasonably accurate view of the future so that the partners can make the correct investments in growth while opportunity windows are still open. In all of these activities, continuity is the key to preventing departnering. A single lapse is not always fatal but "What have you done for me lately?" remains every partnership's acid test.

A supplier who loses sight of the need for continuity becomes a former partner. He has done himself in by not doing his partner right. He has probably taken his eyes off the ball and worked on minor projects rather than the major projects that rank highest on the customer's "must list" for his competitive advantage. Or, if that is not the case, he has lost track of the strike count by failing to recognize how many times the partners have fallen short of the partnership's objectives, especially when the objectives are perceived to be critical to customer success.

Departnered suppliers prove that they have not really been in the game for a long time by their typical reaction of surprise at their departnering. In one form or another, they say, "Just the other day, they were telling me what a great guy I was." In reality, just the other day was probably some time ago. But even if the recollection is accurate, just the other day is still not lately.

Customers are less frequently the cause of departnering. A customer may be uncertain about the original choice of his partner and his lingering doubts may turn into second thoughts after their partnership has gotten under way. Sometimes, after a customer sees that his profits can be improved in a growth partnership, he will seek to maximize them by coveting a potentially more potent partner.

In large part, customers who hold back in their commitment to a supplier partner or who distract themselves by looking around or playing around after they have already allied are reverting to their traditional customer-supplier relationship. They need to be programmed in the mating rites of partnership, in which concentration and dedication are the requirements of allied growth, before they can become satisfactory partners.

Controlling Downsides of Partnering Up

If you are the smaller partner in a small-large alliance, and especially if you are in the common small-company position of being the product supplier in a product-sales alliance, you run the greatest risk of encountering the downsides of growth partnering. With this in mind, you can plan ahead to control potential damage before it occurs by keeping the experiences of other companies in mind.

Fidelity Investments and John Nuveen & Co. are financial services businesses, with Nuveen the smaller and more specialized of the two. They formed a product-sales alliance for Fidelity to market Nuveen investment trust portfolios through Fidelity's retail brokerage chain. The idea itself was not new. Nuveen trusts were already being marketed through other brokers and Fidelity already sold other suppliers' mutual funds. But Fidelity had never before allied with such a major player as Nuveen, and Nuveen had never partnered with a giant business the size of Fidelity. Yet both partners could foresee obvious growth.

Fidelity's retail network and marketing expertise offered expanded sales potential for Nuveen's bonds. In return, Fidelity could obtain an established branded product line to move through its sales network without having to build a new product from scratch. Fidelity could also see the opportunity to position itself as a full-service investment business, going beyond its historic role of being a big name in mutual funds.

If Nuveen's sales fizzled through Fidelity, Nuveen would be hurt more than Fidelity. Paradoxically, Nuveen also stood to lose more if sales were successful. Fidelity has always demonstrated a preference to make and market its own products. Would Nuveen simply be educating a future competitor and paying it for the privilege of learning Nuveen's business?

In thinking it over, Nuveen's speculation on the potential downside from Fidelity becoming a competitive supplier went like this:

The immediate benefits are positive and projectable. Future downsides are not. The benefits are significant for both of us. We believe we can grow Fidelity better with our branded products than they can grow themselves with imitative me-too products. We plan to have our alliance prove that. What if we are wrong? Fidelity will enter the bond business anyway, either with another partner or by itself. Through our growth partnership, the incremental sales that Fidelity makes of our bonds will provide incremental revenues and earnings that will go to us, not someone else. They will expand our markets and add value to our brand name. Even if Fidelity eventually comes out with a competitive product, we plan to retain a significant share of our expanded market. Furthermore, the overall market will be larger.

Polaroid Corporation has gone through much the same thought process. At the end, it licensed the larger Minolta Camera Company of Japan to take over the marketing of Polaroid's most sophisticated instant camera, the Spectra Pro, in specialty photography stores where Minolta is a much bigger player than Polaroid. Polaroid believes that this can stimulate interest in instant photography in the specialty market that it has only thinly penetrated. At the same time, Polaroid can go on selling the Spectra Pro through the big retail camera chains and discount drugstores where it has had its traditional strength.

Minolta sees the partnership in two ways, one of which poses a potential downside for Polaroid. It gives Minolta immediate representation in instant photography. Furthermore, Minolta gets an inside look at the instant photography business without the expense of setting up its own manufacturing facilities and working around Polaroid's patents. It also gets an inside look at Polaroid, from plant to retail.

The Nuveen-Fidelity and Polaroid-Minolta partnerships, both partnering a smaller product maker with a larger marketer, show the comparatively superior strength that marketing partners can always exert, and the threats they can therefore impose, over their product-supplying partners. Marketers command access to a revenue source. Product makers own a costly asset base. Their value is in their brand names. But products are branded only in the minds of markets. Without access to those markets, a brand's value is, either in whole or in part, unrealizable because it remains unmarketable.

Strategic alliances between small and large companies can be high-risk ventures for the junior partner if he puts all his eggs in the large partner's basket. If the principal partner pulls the plug, the junior partner may be left high and dry. Its research will have become focused on satisfying a single user, its production will be dedicated to that customer, and its other customers will be either sparsely developed, poorly served, or nonexistent.

A classic case is Computer Memories Inc., a maker of disk drives that became an IBM business partner. One by one, other customers dropped out because of product and service unavailability. For a while, Computer Memories did not care. Being IBM's primary supplier was enough. When IBM stopped doing business with CMI after a year, the company was reduced to a holding company shell with three employees and stock trading at $1.80 from a one-time high of $32.

On the other hand, five machine-vision manufacturers have been partnered by General Motors. All have achieved short-run gains. Nonetheless, they all live with the knowledge that the GM financing that is supporting their growth is also influencing their research and development, skewing it to GM's needs.

Abandonment is not the only potential problem. In some cases, small companies have been swallowed up without a trace, either being absorbed or suffocated. Exxon Corporation made the mistake of imposing megacorp plans and controls on several high-tech microcorps it had acquired in office automation systems. When Exxon tried to unite them into a single organization, their entrepreneurial spark was squeezed out and their businesses went along with it.

The airlines industry has applied a variation on the Exxon formula to dozens of small regional airlines that have been incorporated into the systems of major carriers either by outright ownership or marketing alliances. Most of the regional lines have been reduced to puppets and have lost effective control of their businesses. Some can neither start nor end service on a route without their partner's approval.

Even when they work out, growth partnerships between small and large companies are never easy. For every ten alliances that agree to talk partnering, eight fail in the discussion stage. A third of the survivors go nowhere even after letters of intent have been exchanged. After the agreements are signed, sealed, and delivered, as many as two-thirds fail to achieve their objectives.

The 33 percent of small companies that successfully ally with larger partners have learned three lessons:

1. Never let a larger partner account for more than 20 percent of total revenues.
2. Never let a larger partner absorb more than 50 percent of total development time, manufacturing resources, or influence on product strategy.
3. Never neglect to cultivate other partners.

9

Profit-Making From Growth Partnering

Product-driven and process-centered businesses think of themselves as making profits by managing their assets cost-effectively. Partnering businesses help manage their customers' assets more profitably. They free up new assets from a customer's current operations by releasing funds from unnecessary costs. They also bring in additional new assets by giving a partner expanded access to funds being used for other purposes by his own customers or spent with other suppliers.

A key question for every partner is, Where are my profits made? The answer predicts the flow of partnered funds and resources, since that is where they will have to be invested. If you say that your profits are made inside your own operations, you are a business introvert who looks at your processes—R&D, engineering, manufacturing, and marketing—as your profit sources. If you say that your profits are made outside your business, in the businesses of your customers who apply your products and services to their own operations, you are a business extrovert who looks at your customers as your profit sources.

Costs are the only result of the actions of a supplier. Profits come from customer action. Partnering offers a strategy for influencing customer action to improve its profitmaking capability and then sharing the improved profits. Each cycle you go through of improving customer profits and sharing the improvement grows your partnership.

A supplier partner will generally have to kick off a growth cycle by putting the ace card on the table. The ace card says three things:

1. We calculate that we can grow you *this much*.
2. We calculate that we can grow you this much *this soon*.
3. We calculate that we can grow you this much this soon *this sure*.

The ace card challenges each candidate for partnership to come up with responses to such questions as:

- ▲ Is the amount of proposed partnered growth significant enough and soon enough to make it compelling for me to partner?
- ▲ Can I obtain this same amount of growth within the same time frame by myself?
- ▲ Can I obtain the same or an even greater amount of growth or obtain it sooner or with greater certainty with another partner?

If the responses to the first question are yes and if the responses to the second and third questions are no, the potential partners are ready to face up to the final hurdle of partnership planning: How can the proposed muchness and soonness of partnered growth be assured? The answer to this question is the business case for partnering.

Value-Basing Your Partnerships

The value of a growth partnership is the cumulative incremental profits that accrue to the "three principals" in every partnership: first and foremost, the customer-partner; then the supplier-partner; and third, the "partnership account" conceived as a third entity. Even if a partnership is not a chartered business such as a joint venture or consortium, it is a useful fiction to treat it as a business in itself. This gives the partners a proprietary sense of belonging to their own enterprise, something that is exclusively *theirs,* and enables them to track the progressive worth of the equity they are building for it.

A partnership's value represents the difference for both partners between doing business as competitive buyers and sellers and working together as cooperative growers. In this sense, the values of each partnership are wholly added values. They accrue over and above the profits that either partner would otherwise have been able to make. From another perspective, partnership profits reveal the opportunity cost of not partnering that the partners have avoided. This would have been money left on the table and lost forever by both of them.

In order to minimize value losses, you should cultivate the habit of exploring each partnership opportunity from two vantage points: how your partner is probably looking at your potential added value and how you ought to look at his.

Value-Basing in Customer Terms

▲ *Value of investing in your business compared to making a similar investment to grow his own business.* How do the returns compare? Which has the quicker payback? Where is the lesser risk?

▲ *Value of investing in your business compared to making a similar investment to be grown by another partner.* How do the returns compare? Which has the quicker payback? Where is the lesser risk?

As a result of each of these calculations, a customer must be able to conclude that a dollar invested to be grown in partnership with you will most likely yield a more desirable return than the same dollar invested in his own business or with another partner.

Value-Basing in Your Terms

▲ *Value of investing in your own business compared to making a similar investment to grow a customer's business.* How do the

returns compare? Which has the quicker payback?
Where is the lesser risk?
- *Value of making a similar investment to grow another customer's business.* How do the returns compare? Which has the quicker payback? Where is the lesser risk?

As a result of each of these calculations, you must be able to conclude that a dollar invested to grow a customer in partnership with you will most likely yield a more desirable return than the same dollar invested in your own business or with another partner.*

These value measurements of partnering are quick screens for making go–no go decisions about a partnership candidate. They also tell you how your prospective partners will quick-screen you. These are "hard" criteria, based on quantitative forecasts of the most likely future value of an investment. Unless the hard values make sense, neither you nor a customer will appear to be a worthwhile alternative investment opportunity for each other.

When the hard numbers check out, then softer criteria can come into play: Are these our kind of people? If not, should we partner with them anyway? What can we lose if a competitor partners with them first?

Proposing Your Partnered Value

A growth partnership is a self-perpetuating series of mutual profit-improvement projects. Each project is proposed in the form of a miniature business case that justifies the profit-making investments required on both sides by the value of their returns. Each project challenges the partners to work together as "parallel processors" of the same strategies in order to achieve mutually beneficial objectives. The parallelism of part-

---

*For a fuller explanation of value-basing, see my book *Competing on Value* (New York: AMACOM, 1991).

nering is its most distinguishing feature. As partners, you do business side by side instead of face to face, in confrontation.

As partners, you will be proposing profit projects to each other all the time. What if we do *this?* Each of you will be challenging the other: How much new profits will it add? What if we do *that* instead? How much more profits can we expect?

A proposal to add value to a partner has five parts:

1. A diagnosis of the business opportunity and a quantification of its current direct costs or the current opportunity costs represented by its prospective revenues and earnings.
2. A prescription for a partnered project that can seize the business opportunity and a quantification of the added values that can accrue to the partners as a result.
3. A cost-benefit analysis to prove where the proposed profits will come from and how they will flow. A model to analyze a one-year project is shown in Figure 9-1. Multiyear projects calculate each year's cash flows according to their net present value as of the startup year.
4. A migration plan for what happens next so that solving one problem or seizing one opportunity can lead sequentially to another without loss of momentum. This enables each partner to maximize his "share of partnership."
5. A control schedule to monitor the project's progress by measuring its results at specific milestones along the project's time frame, and correcting deviations from plan as soon as they occur.

Your value as a partner will be judged by the profits you improve, not by the performance of your products and services that support it. Partnering puts you in the profit-improvement business. Your project proposals must position you as business growers who are experts at working inside or alongside your partner's business operations and whose primary skills are less in making and selling products and more concerned with their

Figure 9-1. Cost-benefit analysis.

Incremental Investment

1. Cost of proposed equipment/system $ _____
2. PLUS: Installation costs   _____
3. PLUS: Investment in other assets required   _____
4. MINUS: Avoidable costs (repairs and re-
    modeling)   _____
5. MINUS: Net aftertax adjustment for sale of
    properties retired as result of investment   _____
6. MINUS: Investment credit   _____
7. TOTAL INVESTMENT (Sum of 1 through 6)   _____

Costs–Benefits (Annual Basis)

	Proposal	Present or Competitive	± Difference
8. Sales revenue	$ _____	$ _____	$ _____
9. MINUS: Variable costs	_____	_____	_____
10. Labor (including fringe benefits)	_____	_____	_____
11. Materials	_____	_____	_____
12. Maintenance	_____	_____	_____
13. Other variable costs	_____	_____	_____
14. TOTAL variable costs (Sum of 10 through 13)	_____	_____	_____
15. Contribution margin (Sum of 8 through 14)	_____	_____	_____
16. MINUS: Fixed costs			
17. Rent or depreciation on equipment	_____	_____	_____

18. Other fixed
    costs   _____   _____   _____
19. TOTAL FIXED
    COSTS   _____   _____   _____
20. Net income be-
    fore taxes   _____   _____   _____

Accounting Rate of Return on Proposed Investment

21. Total investment cost (Line 7
    or total capitalized annual
    costs of system) $ _____
22. Net income before taxes for
    year (Line 20)   _____
23. Before-tax return (Line 22 ÷
    Line 21)   _____ %

application, installation, and implementation to produce results.

Basing Price on Improving Profits

Instead of the operating performance specifications offered by product features and benefits, profit offerings carry financial performance specifications. They tell a partner how much added value he can expect from partnership with you and how soon he can expect it. This becomes his *return.* They also tell him how much he will have to *invest* with you to achieve the proposed return. This becomes your price. Because there will be a return to your partner in excess of what he must put up to receive it, your price is his investment.

Partnering on a return-on-investment basis calls for your proposals to be assessed as support for a partner's financial objectives rather than his purchasing guidelines or operating standards of performance. The assessments of your proposals will accordingly be made by value-sensitive business and financial managers instead of cost-sensitive purchasing managers and performance-sensitive technical managers.

A traditional price must be justified by the unholy trinity of a product's technical performance values, its cost, and competitive prices. An investment is justified by its return: how soon its yield accrues and how much it comes to, compared against similar investments of similar risk. High returns, quick returns, and safe returns justify high investments. When an investment can be paid back quickly, its principal sum plus its profits can be reinvested to start another cycle of investment and return. Once sufficient return has accumulated, each reinvestment cycle can be funded with new profits that have been generated by the partnership itself—"found money" rather than the partners' operating funds.

Because price is a cost, prospective partners will always want to pay less of it. Yet partners will pay the equivalent of a premium price in the form of a premium investment in order to obtain a premium return. This is because their managers, like your own, are used to investing money to make money— not to buy products but to buy money in the form of profits. They are used to putting a value on money in terms of how much it should cost, how much it can be reinvested for in their own business, and the minimal hurdle rate to apply to an investment's return to determine whether or not it constitutes a good deal. They know how to compare one investment opportunity against competitive opportunities and the opportunity costs of delaying their decisions.

The proposal process of partnering sells return on investment and bases the investment on the return. The worth of improved profits, which represent a partner's growth, is being priced. What is it worth, partnered proposals ask, to grow by solving this cost problem or seizing this revenue and earnings opportunity? What is the value they will add to your competitive advantage? What if we can help you achieve it—what is a fair investment?

All growth is good as long as it is cost-effective. Fast growth is better, reflecting the time value of money that makes today's profits worth more than tomorrow's. Safe growth is best. Fast, cost-effective safe growth is a blue chip opportunity. It commands a blue chip investment.

No matter what amount of improved profits you offer, it will never be enough. No matter how quickly you offer them, it will never be soon enough. Partners will always want more profits sooner. This gives you price elasticity, allowing you to move your investment requirements up or back to match each partner's needs for value. No two investments and no two returns are likely ever to be the same.

What-Iffing Your Way to Profits

Growth partners negotiate their mutual value-adding process with each other through a "what-iffing" process. Each asks the other: *What if* we were to do this or that—how much growth would that add to the partnership? *What if* we add this to our strategy mix—or subtract that—or combine this with that; what then?

Partners judge each other by the number and quality of what-ifs they contribute to their partnerships. Each partner should strive for a steady state of high what-if output since every what-if contains a promise of improving the partnership's profits. A low what-if index signals a moribund relationship.

What-iffing is inoffensive. It is an ideal partnership negotiation style since it is devoid of authoritarianism or arrogance. It makes strategy options challenging to consider, not mandatory to accept. Nor does it assume that one partner has a monopoly on ideas for driving the partnership. What-ifs compel interaction. As one idea builds on another, the initiator can progressively add to the value of his suggestions as they eventually become joint properties of the partners whose original authorship can be as difficult to recall as it is irrelevant.

For partners, the best rule to remember is that *you are what you what-if.* Partners need each other for their complementary resources. But the ability to mobilize resources so that their value can be maximized depends on the partners' mutual creativity in provoking each other to question their standard operating assumptions.

Partnering is nonstop what-iffing. When the what-ifs stop, partnership stops because the partners are no longer stimulating each other's growth. What-ifs are the key to growth because they operate on two levels. The first is explicit: try this idea on for size. The second is implicit: I have been thinking about your business and how to grow it.

In what-iffing, each actionable what-if answers the question "What do I need you for?" Here is one more installment of my value, it says. It represents the specific cut I am able to take at our partnership, based on my experience (which is different from yours), my areas of expertise, and my industry culture. How does it look to you? Take your own cut at it. That will give it the benefits of your own particular experience, your own areas of expertise, and your own industry and corporate cultures. Nobody else can put such a combination together. What if we what-if it back and forth to see what happens?

Partners negotiate through what-ifs because the what-if process grows strategies, building one idea atop another to make it a true cooperative method—the essence of negotiation. Since both partners participate, the final strategy will contain inputs from both of them; genetically, it will be a genuine partnered offspring.

What-iffing provides partners with a continuous informal planning process, giving them a heads-up, on-their-toes stance with each other. What-ifs are designed to be interruptive, confronting complacency and predictability. They are calculated to intrude on repetition, doing the same things in the same way just because they have always been done that way. Partners in the act of what-iffing each other are engaged in an unbalancing act to rattle each other's preconceptions about the best ways to grow. If they are not what-iffing, they are not partnering. And if they are not partnering, they are not maximizing their growth.

10

Better Mousetrapping Through Growth Partnering

In the 1980s, when American-made quality was either suspect or patently deficient according to global standards, the Malcolm Baldrige National Quality Award was commemorated to make quality the number one job. As quality has become equality, it now differentiates only by exception to the standard. Without it, you cannot sell; with it, you cannot sell on quality alone either.

For the 1990s, the National Quality Award needs to be paralleled with a National Partnership Award that would go to the businesses that each year have done the best job of helping their customers accelerate growth. Each year's "Growth Partner of the Year" in each industry would have supplied its customer with high-quality profits at a permissible level of 3.4 failures to deliver growth out of every one million transactions. The partnered customer of such a growth supplier would be driven by the supplier to grow. Driving the customer's growth would be the supplier's equal and opposite reaction to being driven by the customer's needs.

A lot will change in companies that elect to partner their growth.

When Paul Allaire became CEO of Xerox, he said, "I have to change the company substantially to be more market driven.

If we do what's right for the customer, our market share and our return on assets will take care of themselves." What's right for the customer is to have his growth accelerated. Allaire believes in giving his people the objective to "satisfy the customer." What satisfies the customer best is his own competitive growth.

Growth partners of the year will have moved upscale from concern that their products are perfect to a preoccupation with the perfection of the growth of their partners. A new definition of perfection based on growth will emerge. So will a new strategy for growth. John Reilly, CEO of Monroe Auto Equipment whose shocks and struts compete in a mature industry, will have cause to reconsider his belief about commodity businesses that "Growth means taking business from someone else." That kind of growth is high-cost, low-margin growth that is more often bought with aggressive pricing than sold. With growth partnering, Reilly's definition can make growth mean "adding profits to someone else"—his customers—rather than taking them from his competitors.

In industries at the other end of the invention scale, where technological innovations come into the market every few months, it is easy to believe along with Phil Knight, CEO of sports shoemaker Nike, that new technologies are the critical success factor in pepping up the market. Ever-new versions of Air Jordans are undeniably one part of the equation. "Air Partners" to sell them in the stores are the other.

Compaq Computer has committed itself to grow through "defect-free products and services." Its name reflects its commitment: an amalgam of computer, compactness, and quality. Yet Compaq is consistently forced to discount its prices by one-third and more because it has not learned how to partner the growth of its customers. Strangely enough, Compaq knows how to partner in its role as a customer if not a supplier. When Compaq needed a hard disk drive for its first laptop computer, it helped finance Conner Peripherals, a Silicon Valley startup. According to Compaq CEO Rod Canion, "We worked so closely with Conner that they were literally an extension of our design team."

No company can keep up a high rate of growth any more

just by making quality products. Without quality partners, they will have no one to produce for. It is impressive for Rubbermaid to set a goal that says, "In any given year, 30 percent of sales will come from products introduced in the last five years." But even though this type of innovation machine may overrun competitors by launching 300 or so new products a year, it is Rubbermaid's retailers who will have to grow Rubbermaid. This makes Rubbermaid's first commandment to grow them.

In the prepartnering days of business xenophobia when companies were closed to partners who were not insiders, most managers approached growth by trying to make more products faster, better, and cheaper than anyone else in their industry. They defined growth in product terms. Andrew Grove, CEO of Intel Corp., exemplifies this point of view when he says, "When your products are the best, you define the game your competitors have to play on your own terms." In reality, it is only if your growth partners are the best—if they are growing you the best—that you can define your game as an end-game for your competitors.

Otherwise you run the risk of becoming Hewlett-Packardized. HP has been described as a font of innovation with 12,000 products that sometimes come up with a solution to a problem that didn't exist. HP's Dick Alberding believes there is such a thing as a "techological inflection point" where the company's many and varied capabilities intersect with unmet customer needs. From its customers' point of view, the inflection point that matters most is where their profit gap from unfulfilled growth may be intersected by HP's capabilities to plug it or, more affirmatively, add to growth by taking their profit curves up another notch or two. This will be accomplished by HP's partnerability, its strategy for growing the customer companies it serves and its peoples' skillsets as business growers, not just technicians.

When growth skillsets are taken apart and examined, they can be seen to contain not only prodigious product development talents or passions for quality but primarily business growth savvy. This is more likely to be expressed in the form of services, not products: services that apply products and implement them in accord with a partner's strategic growth plan, services that inform and educate a partner's people in improving their chances of achieving their plan, and services that counsel them in the best ways to utilize their assets, conserve their cash, control their costs, and expand their profitable revenues.

In the final analysis, growth partnering is more about people than products, more about the quality of added customer profits than enhanced product performance, and more about the best strategy for growing the long-term value of a partner's business than offering the greatest immediate value in a particular product at a particular price.

Pride in making the best has always been a component of leadership companies. Pride in making your customers the best not only ensures a growing market for the best products; it also ensures that you will make a growth profit from the business you do with it. World-class products without world-class growth equals only world-class costs.

Corporate exaltation and national celebration have historically attended products that combine the right mix of sophisticated technology, design, and reliability that enables them to achieve market leadership. Lists of the "One Hundred Best" of these products appear regularly. For many of them, their commercial life cycles turn out to be shorter than their development cycles. Even while they remain major factors in their markets, their asking prices often go unrealized. This should not discourage the pressure for product quality. It should, however, warn against a reliance on it as the magic bullet for profitability in the absence of a high quality of customer growth.

The best cautionary note would be an annual list of the "One Hundred Best Growth Partners," the companies that grow their customers best through a mix of sophisticated management skills in customer operations, recurrent contributions to customer cost reduction and revenue expansion, and reliability that enables their customers to achieve market leadership. To be recognized as a customer grower ought to be the supreme accolade that would make every growth-minded customer in your industry want to do business with you even if, in any given year, you lack one of the one hundred best products.

The better mousetrap is no longer a product. It is the ability to grow a customer. If you build a reputation for having a better value to add to your customers, your own best growth partners will beat the path to your door.

Index

ABB (ASEA Brown Boveri), 22–23
ABC Convenience Stores, 81–82
airline industry, 19–20, 23, 29, 36–37, 130–131
Alberding, Dick, 145
Allaire, Paul, on customer partnering, 143–144
Apple Computer, 2–3
appraisal guideline, 72
ASEA, 22–23
asset turnover, 69–71
AT&T, 18
automobile industry, 3–5, 18, 28–29, 130

Baxter Healthcare Corporation, *xiv*
BBC Brown Boveri, 22–23
Boeing Company, 2, 19–20
bonuses, 44
branding, 39, 76

Canion, Rod, on supplier partnering, 144
cash flow, 6–7, 84
chief executive officers, partnering of, 45–47
Chrysler, 3
Compaq Computer, 144
competition, impact on lead time, 84–85

complementary partners, 15–16
Computer Memories Inc., 130
computers, 2–3, 18, 19, 35–37, 49, 130, 145
concept statements, 116–117
Conner Peripherals, 144
control, structuring partnership, 11–12
control schedule, 137
cost-benefit analysis, 137–139
cost reduction, 26
  partnerability grids for, 53–55
  in prospecting for partners, 56–58
  strategies for, 10, 11
cost tradeoffs, 96
customers
  assessment of partnership, 88
  as cause of departnering, 127
  certifying, as growth partners, 51–56
  optimal mix of, 58–60
  in product development, 91–101
customer-specific growth, 33, 34–37

Daimler-Benz, 28–29
departnering, 12–14, 126–127
development management, 61
Dial Corporation, 31
Digital Equipment Corporation, *xv*, 2, 35–36

Dresser-Wayne, 80–82
DuPont, 75, 98–100

Eastman Kodak, 35–36
European Community (EC), 22
Exxon Corporation, 130

facilities management, 34–37
fads, 94–95
Fidelity Investments, 128–129
financial service companies, 128–129
financial support services, 62
fixed investments, 71
Ford, 3
formidable formulas, 108

Genentech Inc., 18
General Electric Company, *xiv–xv*, 22
General Motors, 3–5, 18, 130
Genex Corporation, 18
grandview criteria, 109
Grove, Andrew, on competition, 145
growth partnering
    buying into, 6–7
    certifying growth partners in, 51–56
    large companies in, 16–17, 19–20, 128–131
    midsize companies in, 16–17, 20–21
    with multiple suppliers, *see* multisupplier partnering
    positioning in, *see* positioning
    small companies in, 16–20, 128–131
    structure of partnership in, 7–12
growth positioning, *see* positioning
growth strategies, 8–11, 89
    creating, 76–78
    for customer mix optimization, 59–60
    mutually participative, 67–68, 70–82

return on investment and, 70–76
    success factors for, 77–78, 79
    targeting partnerable opportunities as, 78–82
growth units, 45

Hewlett-Packard Company (HP), 36–37, 49, 145
hit ratio, joint venture, 104–106

IBM, 2–3, 12, 18, 19, 35–36, 130
incentive guideline, 72, 73
incremental cost, 6
industry-specific growth, 33
information technology, 27
innovation, 145
    growth teams and, 42
    in multisupplier partnering, 17–20
Intel Corp., 145
international partnering, 20, 22–23, 28–29
investment
    intensity of, 77–78
    turnover of, 39–40

John Nuveen & Co., 128–129
joint ventures, 36–39, 103–119
    operating as a venture team, 117–119
    phasing, 115–117
    planning of, 104–106, 117–119
    reward schedules for, 44
    selection procedure for, 106–115
just-in-time production, 2

keyhole criteria, 109–115
Knight, Phil, 144
Kodak, 35–36

lead time, impact of competition on, 84–85
Linda Effect, 12–14, 126
Lufthansa, 23

managers
  in organizational structure for
    growth partnering, 60–65
  partnering by top-level, 45–47
manager-specific growth, 33–34,
    37–40, 45–47
managing accounts, 4
manufacturing, 27, 35
marginal income, 77–78
marketability, of venture product or
    service, 108–115
marketing function, 27
  R&D joined with, 62–64
market makers, 26–28
market penetration, 83
market potential, 83
market share growth strategies, 10–
    11, 78
maturity, 25
McDonald's, 5
MCI Communications, 19
measurement system, 68, 82–85
Metaphor Computer Systems, 18
microbiology, 18
migration plan, 137
Minolta Camera Company, 129
mission statement, *xvi–xvii*
Monroe Auto Equipment, 144
Monsanto, 18
multisupplier partnering, 15–23
  complementary, 15–16
  international, 20, 22–23
  large suppliers in, 16–17, 19–20
  midsize suppliers in, 16–17, 20–
    21
  peer, 16–17, 20–21
  small suppliers in, 16–20
  supplemenatry, 16

National Quality Award, 143
New Venture Gear, 3
Nike, 144
nonproducts, 96–100
Northern Telecom, 49

objectives
  of growth partnership, 8–9
  setting mutual, 67–69, 73–74
Omnical Corporation, 18
organization structure
  for growth partnering, 60–65
  for venturing, 118–119

partnerability
  analyzing, 49–51, 53–55
  targeting opportunities in, 78–82
partnered growth plan, 68, 85–90
partnership investment, 71, 74
partnership profit, 71
partners' sandwich, 108–115
peer partnering, 16–17, 20–21
Philips, 22
Phillips Petroleum Company, 26
planning, 12–14, 67–90
  joint venture, 104–106, 117–119
  measuring achievement in, 68,
    82–85
  mutual objectives in, 67–69, 73–
    74
  mutual strategies in, 67–68, 70–
    82
  partnerability grids in, 53–55
  profit plan in, 68, 85–90
  strategic, 27
Polaroid Corporation, 129
positioning, 25–47, 88
  cost reduction in, 26
  customer-specific growth in, 33–
    37
  facilities management in, 34–37
  growth teams in, 40–45
  industry-specific growth in, 33
  international, 20, 22–23, 28–29
  manager-specific growth in, 33–
    34, 37–40, 45–47
  propositions of, 28–32
  revenue enhancement in, 26–28
  top-level, 45–47
  as value-adding partner, 50–51

predictive guideline, 72–73
price, and profit contribution, 139–141
probability of product acquisition, 84
problem-solving, *xiv*, 121–131
   controlling the downsides of partnering, 121, 128–131
   managing people changes and, 121, 124–127
   mutual trust and, 121–124
Procter & Gamble (P&G), 29–31
product development, *xiv*, 91–101
   codeveloping customer teams in, 100–101
   cost tradeoffs in, 96
   customers in, 91–101
   development lag in, 95
   enoughness in, 93–94
   fads in, 94–95
   nonproducts and, 96–100
   shift point in, 93, 94
product or process technology, 27
product quality, 78
profit contribution, *xiii, xvi*, 26–28, 133–142
   basing objectives on, 68–69
   in decision to work as partners, 58
   focus on, 39–40
   as key to growth partnering, 6–7
   as objective of growth partnership, 8–9
   price and, 139–141
   proposing your partnered value in, 136–139
   supplier role in, 1–2
   value-basing partnerships in, 134–136
   what-iffing and, 141–142
profit margin, 69, 70–71
profit plan, 68, 85–90
profit sharing, 44
progress awards, 43–44
prospecting, 49–65
   analyzing partnerability in, 49–50

   certifying growth partners in, 51–56
   first steps in, 56–60
   maximizing partnerability in, 50–51
   organizing around partners in, 60–65
   partnerability grids for, 53–55

quality, 78, 143–147
quick screen criteria, 114–115

Reilly, John, on growth, 144
research & development, marketing joined with, 62–64
retailing, 5, 29–32, 35, 86
return on investment (ROI) in partnered growth, 7, 9
   basing partnership objectives on, 68–69
   guidelines for, 72–73
   joint venture, 111–114
   limits on, 73–75
   in proposal process of partnering, 139–141
   variables of, 70–71
return potential, 88–89
revenue expansion, 10
   partnerability grids for, 53–55
   positioning and, 26–28
   in prospecting for partners, 56–58
rewards, 73
   of growth partnerships, 8, 10–11, 42–45
   growth team, 42–45
risk, of growth partnerships, 8, 11–12
Rubbermaid, 145
Rubicam, Raymond, on building businesses, *xvii*

sales forecasts, *xiv*
sales management, 62

Scandinavian Airlines System (SAS), 23
Searle, G. D., 18
Sears, Roebuck Inc., *xv*
Sematech, 31
Sherwin-Williams Inc., *xv*
shift point, 93, 94
skunk works, 118–119
Southland Corporation, The, *ix–xii*, 31–32
strategic planning, 27
strategies, *see* growth strategies
structure, partnership, 7–12
    control and, 11–12
    mutual objectives in, 8–9
    mutual strategy and, 8, 9–11
supplementary partners, 16
suppliers
    as cause of departnering, 126–127
    role in profit contribution, 1–2
survival-to-loss ratio, 106

teams, growth, 40–45
    Blue Team for today's growth, 40–42
    codeveloping customer, 100–101
    Gold Team for tomorrow's growth, 42
    joint venture, 117–119
    rewarding performance of, 42–45
technology partnerships, 16, 18, 20, 21
Teknowledge Inc., 18
Toyota, 5
trust, in partnering, 121–124

Unisys, 21
United Air Lines (UAL), 36–37

value-basing, partnership, 134–136
variable investments, 71

Wal-Mart, 30–31

Xerox Corporation, *xiv–xv*, 2, 122–123, 143–144

Young & Rubicam Inc., *xvii*

DATE DUE

DEMCO NO. 38-298